T0353696

The Racial Justice Series
By
Roberto Schiraldi

~

Healing Love Poems
*for white supremacy culture:*
Living Our Values

Unexpurgated*Racial Justice Poetry
with Healing Meditations

Men and Racism:
*The Healing Path*

Post Traumatic Macho Disorder
*The Way Home*

Multicultural Counseling
with Boys and Men:
*A Healing Guide*

~

Awakening With Love
For A Life Worth Living

# Awakening With Love For A Life Worth Living

*A Simple Yet Powerful Guide*
*For A Healthy And Happy Life*

Roberto Schiraldi

**BALBOA**.PRESS
A DIVISION OF HAY HOUSE

Balboa Press books may be ordered through booksellers or by contacting:

Balboa Press
A Division of Hay House
1663 Liberty Drive
Bloomington, IN 47403
www.balboapress.com
844-682-1282

Because of the dynamic nature of the Internet, any web addresses or links contained in this book may have changed since publication and may no longer be valid. The views expressed in this work are solely those of the author and do not necessarily reflect the views of the publisher, and the publisher hereby disclaims any responsibility for them.

The author of this book does not dispense medical advice or prescribe the use of any technique as a form of treatment for physical, emotional, or medical problems without the advice of a physician, either directly or indirectly. The intent of the author is only to offer information of a general nature to help you in your quest for emotional and spiritual well-being. In the event you use any of the information in this book for yourself, which is your constitutional right, the author and the publisher assume no responsibility for your actions.

Any people depicted in stock imagery provided by Getty Images are models, and such images are being used for illustrative purposes only.
Certain stock imagery © Getty Images.

Scripture quotation taken from the Holy Bible, NEW INTERNATIONAL VERSION®, NIV® Copyright © 1973, 1978, 1984, 2011 by Biblica, Inc.® Used by permission. All rights reserved worldwide.

Print information available on the last page.

ISBN: 979-8-7652-5923-8 (sc)
ISBN: 979-8-7652-5924-5 (hc)
ISBN: 979-8-7652-5925-2 (e)

Library of Congress Control Number: 2025900683

Balboa Press rev. date:  01/23/2025

# Contents

## PART I
Personal Love Stories

# PART II
## Loving Self-Care Tool Kit

# Prelude

Our Essence

Is

Love

# Prelude

Living Love

It's what we're here for.

Coming Back Home With Ourselves

Re-Membering Who We Are

With Gentleness and Compassion

# Prelude

What's Love Got To Do With It?

Everything.

# Prelude

**What the World Needs Now**

**Is Love Sweet Love....**

**For Everyone.**

# Loving Grateful Dedication

To You Eileen.....The Love Of My Life

You Are A Mirror Of Love

Deep Inside Me

Now and Always.

# PART I

## PERSONAL LOVE STORIES

~

*Living Love...*
*The Most Fulfilling*
*Of All Adventures*

~

# 1.

# Intro.

Hi.... Welcome. I'm happy for you, that you're choosing to explore more about Love. And, I'm excited to offer you what I've learned, and continue to re-learn...about the Greatest Gift of the Universe........Love. A lot of folks, think it's very blasé, blasé to talk about "love"...very over done, etc. And I certainly know there's been a ton of books written about this topic. So what makes this one unique and worth your time? All of what I share here is inter-woven with amazing blessings, gifts, learnings of what <u>literally has saved mine, and many other lives.</u>

A little about me, to start. I'll offer more in a bit. As I'm sitting here putting the final touches on this offering, I again breathe... and take stock...that in a few weeks I'll be officially entering into my 80th year on this planet. And sooo grate-full to still be alive. This is definitely an incredible miracle! By all rights, should have bought the farm eons ago. And I do feel like I've died many times over during this amazing, yet often perilous thing called my life. And yet, with the help of many wiser than me, and a sometimes shaky... yet ever deepening <u>belief in and relationship with a Higher Power... greater than me, I keep re-choosing....to Live....With ...Love....in my efforts to keep re-claiming the goodness of me, and to keep on keepin on with being a better version of me.</u> So, not real complicated. That's basically it,, and what I've got to offer. If you'd like some more, details and how to's.....please keep readin.

In my mid 40's I became Suicidal.... and made a very difficult Choice to Commit to Live ....in life long recovery...from many "addictions"///unhealthy habitual quick fixes....while simultaneously working as a trauma therapist, supporting many others with their life threatening pain. The commitment to spend the rest of my life in gratitude, learning about how to love me, so I could share that love with others, became my reason for living...real living.

I have stumbled many times....yet....always re-membering... re-connecting...with who I truly am.,..Love, makes all the sometimes treacherous hills and valleys well worth it. I am one of the least perfect people I know....and yet.....I know that each of my "imperfections" are perfect for me....and definitely a gift from the universe to remind me to come back home to my most loving self.

So is my story totally unique? Yes and No. I Am Totally Unique. As I believe Everyone is. And I Am Much Like So Many Millions of others. Again, as I believe Everyone is.

So that's what I have to share initially as an intro.

More about me and my Living Love Lessons to come.

# Whew!....

Never thought I'd write a book about me. Having written other books, mostly about racial justice and healing from trauma, I have shared some personal stuff, when I thought it was helpful, and would better help make the points. So that's what I've decided to do more of here. To put my money where my mouth is...to be more <u>vulnerable</u>...(I'm sweating as I type this),..... to share more about my life, and the principles, learnings, strategies that have been so helpful to me and many others.

Counseling training tells us to be ...professional, to not share personal information, history etc., and keep an "objective" distance so as not to project our own stuff on our clients. As an alcohol and other drug counselor and someone in recovery....I learned from some wonderful role models, that sharing some personal stuff can make it feel a lot easier for others to open up, especially when they are less apt to worry about being judged.

And I'm not here to fix or save anyone... "that's up to you....cause it's your life, not mine". I have always made it clear to my clients, "you are responsible for your own choices....literally..your life is in your own hands ...heart. I offer what has helped me and many others... and I will support you to the max, letting you know if I see warning signs of sabotage etc.,....however it is up to you to make your own decisions, based on what resonates and feels right for you."

So, I invite you Dear Reader to....as we say in 12 Step Program... "take what you want...and leave the rest."

And, back to me.

# A Love Story Begins...

I grew up in Brooklyn, NY, and then East Rockaway, Long Island. I know my parents loved us..me, my younger brother and sister, and did the best they could, given where they came from, and had modeled from their parents. We knew we were cared for,...and were taught many valuable life lessons, for which I am very grateful. Wise ones have said, "we choose our parents, for the lessons we need to learn." And I do believe that...

.....and yet, as with most families. It wasn't perfect. There was violence (not always... however... the looming threat... from which I had nightmares)... alcohol... and divorce... when we were young. Fear was a constant companion for me. I was afraid of commitment, and didn't trust that I could ever have a monogamous relationship....didn't feel it was possible.....and like so many, didn't really have a clue about how to love me and others.

I cheated on my high school girlfriend...for which I always, always felt much guilt, (even after going to a 40th high school reunion to apologize to her, she was very gracious and said,,, "we were young"). So lying and cheating became a "normal" for me in my attempts to honor "committed" relationships, through college, and later through two of my own divorces. I felt so much <u>fear, guilt, shame.</u> I knew I wasn't a bad person..... however I also knew I was hurting people who were only wanting to love me.

I played lots of sports... football, basketball, baseball, and a little track.. throughout high school, college, in the service and after. And while I enjoyed the comradery and team work, always felt different...that I really didn't fit in. People didn't know this,,, because I knew how to blend and please others. Other than a few instances, I always felt, not good enough....and often...even an impostor, fraud....

This also played out in my school work, where I cheated to pass exams..because I never felt smart enough. This continued all through college and into graduate school. One "little" irony here....I was working at the time as coordinator of an alcohol and other drug prevention training program for teams of elementary, middle school and high school students and their teachers and counselors from the eastern region of the state.... the idea being, training teachers and counselors to better support students improving their self-esteem, so they wouldn't "need" to use drugs. Me, with my very tenuous hold on my own self-esteem.

Some other "ironies"/ powerful lessons that I am now so grateful for...even though it took me quite awhile to learn them....With a much respected friend, we started a men's center to support others in being better men...something...I sure needed. I also ran a group home for mentally and emotionally disabled men.... again something I could sure relate to. I worked for a time in a prison with men who were there for alcohol and other drug related crimes.....could have been me easily. And then when I was working for a delivery company, got stopped for speeding and arrested and jailed for possession of marijuana.

While my record was later expunged, it was one of many reasons to feel unworthy, an impostor, a fraud. I couldn't allow myself to feel good about the positive things I was doing.

~

The cheating on exams continued mostly through my doctoral program until I was finally brave enough to commit to studying, one day at a time, in preparation for taking my doctoral comprehensive exams..... I prayed hard...and with each next question when I wasn't sure about the answer....would pause, take a breath...and ask for guidance. And it worked... as I miraculously passed.

**The not feeling good enough, an impostor and fraud....still lives with me today, and comes up from time to time,....like now..as I am choosing to be "visible" and step up and speak my truth. So even though I am not being that lying, cheater person today, the old doubts and fear creep in, and I use it as a wake up call...a time to re-member, and remind myself of who I am today.....today....I Am Love. I Am Honest. This Is My Truth. This is how I choose to Live in each moment. With lots and lots of deep, soothing, comforting breaths of life affirming Love.**

~

We will explore more and more about what this thing called love <u>really</u> is (not just some pie in the sky fantasy), and how we can nurture and grow it for ourselves...for our Life. I thought I had a sense of what love was...but really..

that's all it was...a sense. And now...I know, <u>for sure</u>, what love is...what it means, the <u>core ingredients</u>...and how to put it into action. Because, without the action.....it's just a word....without much substance. "Oh, I love you, I love you...oh yeah...why?...and what does that mean?...what do you love about me?...and how do you show it?...and what do I love about you?...and how do I show it?" We'll definitely explore that... lots to come.

So to continue a little more about my story. I barely graduated from high school, and only, because a compassionate, very smart schoolmate let me cheat off of her paper during our final exam (I also apologized to her at the same reunion, to which she responded, "I'm glad I could help, look how well you've done", which helped me feel a little better, still not great). My father, in his wisdom, had me work in construction during the summers, and I quickly realized that wasn't how I wanted to spend my life.

I was barely accepted in college, and again basically, cheated my way through. In my senior year I volunteered to work weekends at a home for emotionally disturbed youth from Brooklyn and Queens, and for one of the first times, felt like I was doing something that actually mattered...and that, just maybe I could help others, who might feel like I did. I also took a course about marriage and the family, and started to realize why I felt like I did, and that maybe, just maybe, there was some way out of the trap I felt stuck in.

It was during the Vietnam War, and even though my dad was a WWII veteran, both my parents were trying to help me avoid being drafted. My mom sent an application for me to Teacher Corps (like a domestic Peace Corps, only working with inner city youth who were struggling to make it in school). I could relate to the kids, so found it worthwhile. While living with some other Teacher Corps interns, I did a huge about face. I went from being a jock, who wanted to be a Special Forces Green Beret for duty, "honor," country to prove my manhood etc.,.. to protesting the war.

However, I was eventually drafted.

My Loving Brother Glenn, who was at West Point at the time, did this incredibly loving thing of coming to Canada with me, to support me, as I was considering the choices between staying in Canada, going to jail, or learning how to kill or be killed. I was so scared, and so angry, I ended up calling my brother a fascist for being part of the war machine. I hurt him greatly, and while I apologized much later, have always felt terrible about how much I hurt him. While I was up there in Canada, I was coached by the resistance office I went to, and learned I could go back and sign up for an extra year (draft was a two year service "commitment"), which would allow me to choose the branch of the service, and be able to be in the Army Medical Corps, so I could help people instead of kill people.

First I went through 8-week Basic Infantry Training, then Combat Medic Training, then Neuro-Psych Training, which prepared me to work in an Intensive Care Psychiatric Care Unit with the guys who were suffering from PTSD (although we didn't call it that back then, we just thought it was run of the mill combat trauma). Didn't learn til many years later, that most of the guys were suffering from intense guilt and shame about the atrocities they either witnessed or committed themselves, like killing, mutilating, raping women, children, innocent people, usually under orders, so were definitely not able to talk about it since they'd be betraying the military/government secrets. Many of those guys ended up either committing suicide or homicide. And like many others, that is when I got into drugs to help me deal with the second- hand trauma, hatred, fear, sadness, grief, and being part of a war machine I wanted no parts of, thus unwillingly contributing to the war effort.

While I was in the neuro-psych training, my buddy and I would sneak off the post and go to an American Friends' office that let us use their printing press, to print a newsletter with letters from the guys in combat about the atrocities we were committing. Of course, we weren't allowed to do that, so the drugs "helped" with the fear of being caught and imprisoned. That's when I also started writing poems, some about my then concept of love, to help me stay somewhat sane during a totally insane period.

I got married while in the service, at age 23, to be able to have legal/consensual sex. I had been a guilt laden "good" Italian Catholic boy, who through many, many "confessions," was committed to being a virgin when I got married. So we had great drug aided sex, while I tried to convince my wife to have an "open" marriage, and I continued to cheat. I was petrified of being a dad, because I didn't feel it was possible for me to be a good parent. The guilt of hurting my wife with my cheating, weighed on me, and I did more drugs. We got divorced after two years.

So for the next 10 years I sewed my wild oats. Continued with the drugs and sex..... and was responsible for at least one abortion that I know of, with a good friend who I had been dating for awhile. I didn't feel worthy or capable of being a responsible parent, and I knew I didn't want to bring another unwanted child into this world. Since abortion was illegal at the time, she had an illegal one, and then we had to rush her to the hospital and lie that she had a miscarriage. Again, much guilt about hurting another good person who I really cared about. Another very significant decision that weighed heavily on me....and for which I felt I could never forgive myself.

After taking some time away from dating, I eventually met another really good person. After dating for about a year or so, we decided to get married, and I decided to really "commit." She had a 14 year old daughter, so I became an instant step-dad. I figured maybe, having a family, would help me to be a responsible "adult." I was determined to "honor" my commitment to be a "faithful" husband and loving stepdad.

My commitment to monogamy lasted for a short time, eventually leading me through many drug hazed incidents, which I felt so much shame and guilt for, that after 10 years of hurting them, ....**I finally decided to <u>commit suicide</u>.** The plan was to pay someone to kill me, so my wife and stepdaughter would get the life insurance pay out (which they wouldn't have if I killed myself),....I called a private detective out of the yellow pages (because I figured they were all slime buckets), and offered him $2000. which was all I had in the world... and after a silence, he said "No I won't kill you, and you need to go get help".....("Chester Springs Detective" later on, is the poem about that).

I eventually got into an intensive care treatment program for folks from "dysfunctional" / traumatic family backgrounds. And that's when I had to make a decision...

...live or die...again. Only this time, I knew it was the last draw. It was all on the line. The two amazing wise, powerful women who ran the program didn't mess around. I was either gonna make a <u>full-on 100% commitment to sobriety, and 100% integrity</u> .......or they wouldn't waste their time, as they had too many folks whose lives were on the line. They carefully explained about and gave me a <u>suicide / self-care contract,</u> (version of which appears later, and which I give to all my clients...as suicide is a relative term, and even if we don't put a gun to our head, we can kill ourselves slowly with all the unloving decisions we make...continually giving a big middle finger to ourselves in the mirror). So after taking the time to really consider the implications, and knowing, at least, somewhat, how excruciatingly scary and painful the process was going to be, I did the bravest thing I could do. I signed up and eventually made the full-on **"commitment"...to be 100% honest...and to face ....all my greatest fears....especially the fear of learning how to love myself (since I felt like** such a slime bucket, I didn't see how if was possible, to forgive myself, and actually learn to love myself.)...and to eventually, hopefully even be able to share that love.

During this time, we ended the marriage (my wife wasn't willing to go into treatment with me, which I sure couldn't blame her for). **So I figured that was it for me...and I might not be in another relationship for a long time...if ever.**

That ten year or so journey in treatment led me to ....freedom. While I was relieved to finally have all the secrets out...(that had been choking the life out of me...literally almost killing me)..it took a good chunk of time (**some teachers and my experience.... have taught me, it can take between 3-5-10 years, depending on the amount of trauma from our childhood, and how old we are / how long we've been hooked on our less than loving thoughts, words, behaviors (old habits can die hard),** with lots and lots of intensive healing work... to really start feeling significantly better)...(***For a wonderful book on healing from childhood trauma, please see 'The Adverse Childhood Experiences Recovery Workbook,' by my brother Glenn R. Schiraldi***). Understanding more about my background and the emotional impact....and getting a lot of fear, rage, grief.. out, and making the commitment to be completely honest in my recovery efforts helped a lot.

And little by little, I started to believe that I could really live this way....it was possible.....and then.....learning how to forgive myself, and others.

Finally...slowly....gradually.... I started feeling "worthy" of love....kept learning how to actually treat myself lovingly. And eventually started having some sense of what it might feel like to share that love with another (although I still didn't believe that a committed love relationship with another human being was in the cards for me....I at least didn't shut the door to that possibility).

So I kept putting one foot in front of the other.... "one step at a time".....as we say in recovery rooms....and continue.. to keep on keepin on....with this never ending journey of learning about how to get better and better at loving.... accepting, appreciating and respecting ...me....and as a result....better able to share that love with others.

~

Many of the principles and strategies I learned then, and continue to learn ..and re-learn...a never ending growth process...especially with this thing called Love....fill these pages. I am one very blessed, grate-full man.

~

# Another Love Story Begins

In the ensuing years after entering treatment, I eventually met an amazing human named Eileen Gallagher. (She was Coordinator of the Community Gardens Program for the Pennsylvania Horticultural Society, where she would work with inner city, low income, Black and Brown communities in Philadelphia, fixing up abandoned lots, and creating beautiful gardens for growing sustainable organic foods, and for safe gathering places especially for the children and elders of the community. She earned trust and respect. And a couple of her close friends who she worked with in the community invited her to stay with their relatives in Puerto Rico, and Costa Rica. This helped with learning more about cultural customs and traditions, which guided the creation of the gardens back in Phily).

Eileen had been a pre-Olympic swimmer, so smooth and graceful to watch her swim, and a mad hiker, who climbed most of the highest peaks in the country.

There was an ease in being together.

When we would walk ...especially later, on the tow path, through the woods, along the canal.....I would need to jog to keep up with her fast walk. And then we'd pause and sit on our favorite bench. And look at the turtles, fish, frogs, birds,..and she'd always know a tree or plant's name and history when I asked.

We liked to dance..to Sade...especially to one song in particular..... "No Ordinary Love",....hmmm ..wonder why.

While knowing we had an instant mutual attraction, Eileen and I also knew to be wary and take it slow, as we had both been through prior marriages, and didn't want to make similar mistakes. And we both knew we weren't ready.

We stayed good friends over many years, finally, after 35 years, she called one day and said... "I ended the relationship I was in, gave myself a year to heal the wounds / learned the lessons........what do you think?". To which I took a breath (I think) and said... "What do I think?..... I think I've been waiting 35 years, is what I think."......So we started getting together, and eventually discussed what commitment would look like.... what we required of ourselves and each other.....and the bottom line was...

the same for both of us.....100% all in commitment (or else what was the point)....guided by 100% integrity...(no secrets, no little "white' lies etc., because we both knew that those secrets, and so-called little white lies, resulted in laying next to a stranger we no longer trusted).

As we spoke about commitment, and what we meant by "Love", we realized that we both had "accepted" and let go of the fantasy of the ideal love, and had embraced the commitment to Being Alone With Ourself...and were both happy and healthy and enjoying our lives (please see the Marriage Prayer later on). That made the decision to explore being together, one of choice, not necessity or desperation. She knew everything about me...

my darkest secrets....and yet, <u>accepted</u> me. "I know who you really are, and I respect the man you are now." That was one of the most important keys. We both <u>respected</u> each other. An essential aspect of Love. The <u>connection</u> was, and is, on going. We <u>chose to trust</u>, after <u>demonstrating our dependability</u>, over and over. We knew we had each other's backs....

And that deep connection with her....helped me better connect with all other life.

Things seemed to flow better, and make more sense.

All things ...<u>connected</u>...all related....All One.

~

In this midst of us <u>committing</u> (we hadn't planned on moving in together, as we both liked our own spaces),....and yet..... <u>the Universe interceded.</u>....and Eileen got cancer. She had to go through aggressive chemo and radiation, which was excruciating...and kicked her butt. And she's a warrior, not given to complaining, just takin care of business....however it really took it's toll on her. I moved down with her to help take her to treatments and help care for her.....(she lived outside of Phily, in a little love nest that used to be her grandparents', and she would stay there as child and be so happy, felt so loved... lots of woods and animals). The chemo and radiation started effecting her memory, and she was no longer able to adequately care for herself. So I didn't think about it twice, it was clear.... I just told her I wanted her to move in with me....it was so painful for her to have to leave her love nest. And yet it was beautiful to be together.

We had many, many sweet, sweet moments. Didn't have to be "doing" anything particular. Mostly just hangin with each other...enjoying each others' company.

Eileen was always a great support to me and my racial justice and trauma counseling work. If I needed to talk...she'd often stop what she was doing and really hear me. Or asked for some time, and then we'd talk. And I did the same for her. She was... and still is...my best friend.

We continued to go for beautiful walks along the tow path by the canal, and sat by "our" bench. And to another lake I still go to weekly....to be with her. Whenever I see a big winged bird gliding on the wind currents, I know it's her, smiling down on me.

It wasn't perfect. I wasn't always the best care giver. Sometimes I would get impatient...stupid little things ...like I'd share something with her....and a few minutes later she'd ask me the same question...the memory .....or she'd put things away in the kitchen, and I couldn't find them...the memory.....she'd let me know if I was being mean....and I kept working on doing better....For the most part....we were as happy as we could be... considering her suffering.

Her treatment team...were angels of mercy...so kind and compassionate.

And we would sit out on our porch and savor the big trees and soft breezes, and she would say something...and I would crack up. I always smile when I think of her...when I look at her pictures. I miss her like crazy. And sometimes, I still cry. I think the laughing and crying....will be part of me til my last breath. How could it not be. I miss her like crazy.

And she seemed to be doing better, and then.....bam.......we both get covid... then she gets... pneumonia... then... diagnosed with terminal lung cancer... and given 3 months to live. She, very reluctantly, decided to try immuno-therapy which gave us another 9 months together...until finally she'd had enough. And fortunately, here in New Jersey, we have the compassionate endings law where folks who have a terminal disease can die in the privacy and dignity of their own home. She definitely didn't want to be in the hospital, so that is what we did. Many folks breathe their last breath shortly after the medication is administered. I laid there in our bed with her for 5 hours after the medication was administered, holding her, until she finally passed. The doctor said, "She wasn't ready to go yet." Yep, in true Eileen fashion, she had to do it in her own time and readiness.

I miss her like crazy. And had often told her I wanted to go with her...didn't want to be here without her. She said... "It's not your time...you still have more to do here." A few months later it was New Year's ...and I felt it important to make a decision....was I gonna keep on living......and if so...why.....and the answer was clear... "to keep on Living Love...and Sharing that Love...that is why I'm here."

Writing this book, is perhaps, one, if not the most important reasons. And the wind is howling outside, the huge branches swaying...the wind saying.... **"This is why you are here, to write this....Re-member who you are....You Are Love."**

~

# Preliminaries

<u>So why this title</u>.....'Awakening With Love, For A Life Worth Living'

**<u>Awakening</u>**......because for me....I was <u>sleep walking</u> through much of my life.....i.e., looking for "love" in all the wrong places... basically because I was clueless about what love really was. Re-awakening...with Love.....breathing in who I truly am....in me... part of me...my Source...my Highest Self.....connected and re-connected...and re-connected with the Greatest Power in the Universe...Love.

**<u>With Love</u>**.....because it it the main reason I'm still alive and breathing. <u>My choice to keep living</u>, hinges on my commitment to keep learning and growing more and more with Love.

**<u>A Life Worth Living</u>**...That is the choice I made...and continue to make every day......as I remind myself ... "I Am Love."

**<u>Happy and Healthy Life</u>**...If we consistently live by our most loving values..health and happiness will follow. "It's not always easy," (as one of my many teachers told me). However, with choosing love as our constant companion, we will always be able to return back home.. to our natural healthy and happy selves. Much more on this to follow.

# Six Initial Guiding Principles
# To Live And Love By

(Much more on each of these and others, to follow)

**(Honoring Commitment to Keep Becoming Better and Better at Living With)**...

1. **Being Compassionate With Ourselves...With Myself...** Learning how to Be tender... and gentle.... and kind ...<u>with ourselves,</u> first and foremost....otherwise...

we certainly won't be able to be very congruent with sharing that compassion with others, because it will be coming from a hollow place.

...hard to share, what we don't have much of.

Gonna stop here for minute, to share a story (which will likely come up again later on...as it is a crucial piece of my Love journey).

Many years ago....a wonder-full teacher of mine....Tom Balistrieri taught me one of my first lessons about **compassion**. Tom had been a long time apprentice of Joe Eagle Elk, a very respected and revered Iyeska / Medicine Healer of the Sicangu Lakota People, on the Rosebud Reservation in South Dakota. (I was very blessed to be invited to the Rosebud for many years to participate in supporting a 12 day traditional ceremony for peace and healing called Sundance). As I was about to enter one of my first sweat lodges (a low circular dwelling formed by long curved branches stuck in the earth, covered with tarps, and a hole/fire pit in the center where hot rocks from the nearby fire are brought in and water is poured over them to create very hot, cleansing steam, for healing songs, prayers, stories...safe and deeply healing)......a much much longer story...(another point worth noting.....before entering the lodge, I would kneel down and kiss the earth and say "Mitakuye Oyasin"...which is Lakota for "All My Relatives...All My Relations....We Are All Connected....All One", which for me...set the tone for Being with Me...and the others, maybe ten other folks,,, and the Ancestors/Healing Spirit Energy....).........anyway...as I was about to enter...Tom stopped me and said.... "Roberto....you're such a good man....but you're very very hard on yourself.....you need to learn how to be <u>compassionate</u> with yourself."

I was stunned. No one had ever said anything like that to me.... at least that I can recall. And I had been a therapist, and in therapy,...for a long time prior.

Maybe, I just wasn't <u>ready</u> to hear it before (ahh... <u>Readiness</u>.... changing ourselves, doesn't usually happen until we're ready... more about being ready.. to come). Anyway....that sure has stayed with me......**and re-membering to be compassionate with myself.**.... continues to be one of the most important elements of my own healing.......and usually is one of the core elements for most of my clients.....and for that matter....most of the folks I meet on this life journey.

But as many wise ones say, sometimes the most important lessons.....take awhile......

(Everything here,...interconnects....as it sure is hard, if not impossible to love ourselves, or anyone or anything else.... without deep compassion)......

***(Please see the enlightening Ted Talks, and You Tube Videos by Brene Brown on Compassion, and Vulnerability)***

A couple of Compassion poems to follow.....

# Compassion

For me
For others.

For me.
For others.

For me.
For others.

For me.
For others.

Without me,
There is no
Other.

Without the other,
There is no
Me.

Please help me
Remember.

FRS/7/09
(Remembering)

# Compassion 2

I have
deep, deep empathy
and appreciation
for me....

(and am affirming to myself.....and you)

for all I give....
for all you give...

for my caring.....
for your caring.... for the pain of the world

for honoring all of my commitments
for you honoring all of your commitments

I love me....I love you

I appreciate me.. I appreciate you

I comfort me... I comfort you

I respect me... I respect you

I am grateful to me for listening
I am grateful to you for listening

I am with me ......I am with you......
                                    always.

There is no need to keep running...

The struggle is over.....

all....is.....well.

FRS/6/16/15, revised 12/8/24

So back to some of the core Love Principles...

2. **Learning How to Love**..(i.e., Living by core ingredients of what love is... a la, **bell hooks**, in her important book **'All About Love'** (like mutual respect, acceptance, compassion, honesty, trust..etc.,, much much more to come, especially in the "All Life Is Sacred Proposal")).... How to Live Love./ Love in Action....Daily / Moment to Moment Check-ins, Mantra...Breathing in" All Is Well / Breathing Out... "I Am Love"....Breathing / Meditation / Prayers...

3. **//Forgiveness**...Again, Being tender and gentle and kind with ourselves and others, after deep consideration, how I contributed to hurt, what I can do differently, perhaps making amends, (except when to do so would further hurt self or other, (from 12 Steps, and peace makers throughout history)), and sharing how I plan to change the behavior, and then demonstrate that over time....otherwise "sorry" is hollow.

# The Great Apology

My teachers
taught me....
most apologies
ain't worth
the paper
they're printed on.

Talk is cheap
and oh so easy,
automatic,
knee jerk...

"I'm sorry",
"I'm so sorry".

"Oh yeah?...
Show me".

First by acknowledging
the behavior.

Then...by demonstrating
you've given it some
deep consideration
and come up with a plan
to demonstrate

willingness,
and commitment
to change
the behavior.

If not....
please....
save your breath.

--------------------

So these days
I rarely say
"I'm sorry".

And only
after
lot's of consideration.
As to why
and what
I'm willing
to commit
to doing differently.
And what's my plan.

Then, yeah,
maybe then,
After looking
at my motives

with humility
with compassion
with impeccable integrity.

Then maybe,
"I'm sorry".

3/ 2020

# Forgiving

Creator
forgive them
for they know not
what they do.

Creator
forgive me
for I know not
what I did.

Princeton
Hitler
Viet Cong
Wall Street Bankers

As I judge them
So I am judged

Please help me.
Give me all the compassion
forgiveness, humility, love, wisdom
courage I need.

Today I choose
to ask for
and Be
forgiven.

So I
can give
others
the same.

So I can be
the best man
I can be.

To help
make
this world
a more loving place.

If I hold on to the violent
thoughts feelings....
I perpetuate them...
and send more
out to the universe...
and make the world
a more violent place.

May I be Free
of pain and suffering

May all beings
be free
of pain
and suffering.

Please let it be so.

Loyola Retreat.

# Forgiveness

A loving gift
I choose
to give
myself
or the other.
Not prematurely,
as in a "should,"
or because of guilt
or fear.
Then it doesn't ring true.
And then it festers.

Only after honoring
the feelings
the anger
the rage
the hurt
the pain.

And providing
loving comfort
and reassurance,
and whatever else
I need
to feel safe, secure,
solid.

Then, I can choose
to forgive cleanly
to relieve myself,
to free myself

from the darkness
and poison inside.

To come home
to living
in Love.

3/20

More Guiding Principles.....

4. **Fear / Vulnerability**......Being Courageous enough to be **Vulnerable,** which is necessary for real love.

This is a piece from my 'Men and Racism' book....which focuses on being brave enough and compassionate enough to walk through our **fear....of being vulnerable**.....ahh the incredible gifts that follow..if we do.

**FEAR.........**Back to the beginning.....Some views and stories about Fear..... the Sacred....and Love.

**FEAR Intro.....**we live in a .... "Culture of Fear" with ...violence, wars, economic stress, poverty, wars, climate change, insecurity and mistrust .......surviving..... rather than thriving ... with Fear Based Values Systems... get more, better than, more powerful then, protect what "we own".... "Ruling" our world.

**FEAR-** Fear can be seen as a normal response to a one time and/ or persistent stressor. However it can even lead to immobilizing or disabling us, if we don't address it. And.. it can also be viewed as a wonderful signal...a wake up call, if you will, that loving action is needed. **Loving action is always the great antidote for fear.** Loving action will provide reassurance, comfort, relief. All by responding with the simple, yet so powerful question......." **What would love do now.?..... "What would be the most loving thing I can do for myself in this moment?" (from Neal Donald Walsch, in his 'Conversations With God' book series). It will often be a little voice, from deep inside.** So we need to practice, gently quieting our noisy, often distracted minds, with calming, soothing breaths, to really hear this freeing, life giving, life affirming...loving response ("Mindfulness Meditation," developed by Jon Cabat Zinn, is a an example of a simple, wonderful practice that helps us to objectively observe and acknowledge, thoughts, feelings, sensations, sounds, and gently, return "home" again...to breath. It is a regular part of my daily, morning, evening, and whenever I need it, self care practice).

F.E.A.R....FALSE EVIDENCE APPEARING REAL. That's the acronym I learned eons ago from from two wise, strong women who became my trauma therapists for my own initial healing work.

SO WHAT IS THIS GREAT LIE?....THE FALSE EVIDENCE APPEARING REAL LIE?......

SO MANY LIES WITHIN THE LIE.....i.e., lie # 1. we are born lacking....and lie #2...our worth needs to be demonstrated, by lie # 3. accomplishing and lie # 4...accumulating.. and on and on....and it's never quite good enough, so we have to keep on doing more and more and more ...in a never ending battle to prove ourselves worthy enough.... smart enough, strong enough, wealthy enough, powerful enough,....and the never ending war drum keeps beating. Please be clear here....I'm certainly not saying it's not ok to set goals and accomplish, and accumulate...(within reason...as long as Sacred Love is the guiding light we live by (much more about that to follow)..... and basics like ....food, clothing, and shelter are equitably available for all).

And this War thing......

War against who?...against what?......hmmmm......could it be....
ourselves?

And the lie that.... they are "different". "those people". Again,
a seeming oxymoron......for we Are each unique / different.......
and yet, each the same I.e, have the same needs.... for food,
clothing, shelter, safety, "security", caring for and protecting
our loved ones, feeling appreciated and worthwhile....

So yes......we've "been had, took, hoodwinked, bamboozled,
led astray"......often by <u>bullies</u> ...who want to feel better about
themselves, because of their own insecurities, so they convince
themselves that the "differences" of race and ethnicity, gender,
sexual orientation, class, animals, the earth, etc. ......are a
threat, something to be "feared"...not loved...and even "less
than, expendable, disposable". And then they use those lies to
"elevate" themselves into positions of power, wealth, control,
elitism, entitlement, authority / superiority...

and yet.....and yet......
this can also be viewed as ........

...a beautiful opportunity for connection......back "home" with
ourselves.....and with that.... the desire to connect with others.

If we are willing to look deep within, beyond the surface lies,
and many attractive distractions......we can use this awareness
of the similarities as the ticket to freedom.....free from so much

of the alienation that separates us from each other......and most hurtfully.....from ourselves.

As Gabor Mate teaches us in his wonderful video, '**The Wisdom of Trauma**'.....**the greatest trauma is to be alienated from ourselves**.

And that stems from not being taught and modeled and cared for in a way that teaches us ....about All Life Being Sacred...and that each of us is Sacred....and Worthy of Love.

Another Story from this section...

So Back to My Beloved Eileen. And **a story of Sacred, Love, Fear, and Being Vulnerable**.

Eileen was, and always will be, The Love of My Life. She passed five months ago, yet is still very much <u>alive inside me</u>, and always will be. While the pain often feels sooo deep....and a wise one reminded me recently, that the deepness of the pain is a reflection of the deepness of the Love. And I will always feel so Blessed that she chose to Love me. She taught me how to Live Love......how to put the Sacred...and Love...into action.... by offering me unconditional love and acceptance....so that, along with my own commitment to learn how to love me, and to share that love with all life, I finally felt brave enough to ....make a 100%, all out / all in commitment to 100% impeccable integrity with another being....by being....yep...... completely .....VULNERABLE!

~

**So we were walking, hand in hand, as we often did, along the Tow Path next to the Canal.....when...<u>Love and Fear collided inside me.....and I collapsed crying on the ground</u>. Eileen knelt down and held me...gently asking...."What's wrong Roberto?" When I was able to collect myself....I shared with her, what I had never done with anyone else in my life (and I had been married twice before).....that <u>I was scared to death/life of losing her</u>. If she drove back to Phily and got killed in an "accident"...I would be devastated...and didn't**

know if I could go on. That's when I knew...undeniably... felt it ...to the deepest core of me.......LOVE ....and the FEAR....of BEING ....VULNERABLE......YET WITH THE CERTAIN KNOWLEDGE THAT I HAD GIVEN MYSELF THE GREATEST GIFT IN THE WORLD...... LOVE..... <u>Choosing to lovingly face the fear and the risk of losing her</u>...and the love we co-created, by our mutual spiritual commitment to ourselves and each other.....was and will always be....<u>my single greatest accomplishment.</u>

Was I and were we...**perfect**? Hell / Heaven ...NO!.... There was a lot of rough going....especially since I am such an imperfect human with many, many imperfections.

However, as they say.....we were and are perfect together.... because we did our best to honor our commitments to the ingredients of Love, (more about the ingredients of Love, a la bell hooks and her book 'All About Love' later in the All Life Is Sacred section.)

And when we fell short, because we are both very human... we did our best to prevent any drama..... and to acknowledge and understand what happened, what our plan to change was, and do our best to carry through. One of our many great gifts together.

# Vulnerability and Strength

First off..... as I am taking a deep breath.......I need to identify myself as a primarily hetero white male ("pseudo" white male, to be more correct, as I have always related more to being "ethnic" rather than white, and "primarily" hetero, since I relate more to being Two Spirit... more on both later). Yet given all the privileges that I have with this lighter color skin, and not having to fear being persecuted for my gender identity, I feel it's necessary to identify as hetero white male.

And I feel the need to acknowledge .....that it's a whole lot easier for <u>me</u> to be talking about being "vulnerable", when I don't have to feel subjected to the overt, personally directed threat of racism every day of my life.

I have had some men of color respond negatively to my talk of vulnerability. "Yeah, easy for you to say, you don't have to be worried about being profiled". Or, "There is no way I'd teach my son to be "vulnerable", in a society that already treats us like second class citizens".

Ok....so that's what I initially wanted to say.

And... next...... let's ..please.. be clear. <u>Vulnerability,</u> as we are discussing it here....is <u>..**not** ..about weakness or being taking advantage of, running from bullies, allowing ourselves or those we care about...to be intimidated, hurt, etc.....especially from those using their racism, sexism, homophobia, transphobia,</u>

classism, xenophobia, or any other excuses to dis-respect others.

This is one of 5 short stories from that same piece......

A wonderful father of two young Black boys from another country, spoke to me about his challenges, in raising two strong, honest, brave, young men.....yet with the highest priority being.....them not losing their inner "soft hearts" in reaction to a world which was often a "hard" place. Again, a seeming dilemna. ... and / or..an opportunity to model strength and gentleness as complementary....and on the road to real freedom and empowerment.

"Soft Hearts"....melted mine. Stopped me dead / alive in my tracks....brought tears to my heart....time stopped ...in this precious moment....I was re-awakened......the wind howling outside my window....reminds me......This is the Ticket....a Brave Compassionate Soul..wanting to share that with his Young Ones.......

breathing.........

LOVE....LOVE.....LOVE.......…................wow.....wow....wow.....

This is a poem from the same book......

# Vulnerability,

**the antidote
to wealthy,
white,
hetero
male
supremacy**

Since the time
of our ancestors,
the cave "men",
we males learned
to view everything
with **suspicion**,
**hatred**
and **fear**...
keeping the softness
of love
buried
deep inside,
protected
in suits of armor
and wealth.

We've all
been duped...
to be alienated...
from ourselves...
and each other.

To see ourselves
and each other
as **threats...**

instead of
as supportive,
compassionate,
nurturing,

beings
of light
and love,

Beings
who are
**trust worthy.**

**This Original Fear
of all others**
is the foundation
of racism,
and all the other
"isms",
and intentionally
prohibited
"We The People"
from ever
truly meaning
"All the People"....
never really
intended

to apply to
women,
children,
sexual orientations,
refugees,
races,
ethnicities,
abilities,
classes,
animals,
the land.

The good news!
We now have
the opportunity
to truly "evolve",
by embracing
our true wisdom,
and strength,
to be gentle,
and kind,
and brave enough,
to be openhearted,
and vulnerable..
to feel deep love.

This willingness..
to risk..
being hurt,
is the essence

of real growth,
real love,
real men,
healthy humans.

5. **Grieving**-especially with loss of loved one, the depth of our Grief, is a reflection of the depth of our Love. Each tear is a drop of healing. Without tears, we are walled off, constrained, dis-connected from our love. Also, for the deep sadness of how we treat ourselves and each other...(which hopefully motivates to treat ourselves and each other even more compassionately).

## Fear of Tears.... or......Honoring Our Tears.....A Truly Radical Path to Healing

**I know this is a dicey issue for most of us. So please bare with me as we gently traverse what I believe to be one of our greatest paths to healing.**

Hmmm...why is this such an uncomfortable topic? What are we so afraid of?.......

........we'll be called a baby...wimp.....weak....a girl ... and on and on. We'll just be a deep puddle of tears....and never get out of it to be the strong person we need to be.....

........or we'll just be giving in to our weakness, and never do what we need to do to protect ourselves from all the threats <u>out there</u>......

....(or is it really .........<u>in here</u>.....in us?).

Or you might say...."I'm not afraid of my tears....I just don't have any." And yeah..I get that. And........that's sad...and maybe more than a little scary. We men have been taught to not cry.

"Stop crying, or I'll give you something to really cry about". While it may sound contradictory.....I have gratefully learned... that a major part of happy lives, and emotional health....can be our connection to, and celebration of, our tears (which, of course, can also be tears of joy).

When we wall off from our tears....we wall off from a precious part of our hearts.....we learn to hide behind a suit of armor... to protect ourselves from being "vulnerable"...to all the other "threats in our lives".....we cut ourselves off from ourselves, and deprive ourselves of one of the most important, powerful, and essential aspects or our humanity ...of Being an emotionally healthy, balanced...both strong and gentle....real man (real men Do cry)..... (Again..in his powerful video, 'The Wisdom of Trauma', Gabor Mate teaches us, the greatest trauma is the trauma of being alienated from ourselves....from our own tears).

The importance of tears as a pathway to healing cannot be overlooked. We don't just get over childhood trauma, by just wishing it away. The wounds stay buried, deep inside our minds, our emotions, our bodies....each cell, each molecule, each organ....festering....hurting us more and more......until we finally start tending to them. "Just get over it....be a man....that was then...move on,"
doesn't work.

Until we take the necessary time to do the healing work, we won't heal. And the longer the wounds go unattended.....the longer it takes to heal. <u>Our tears can be such a great, soothing balm for our pain.</u>

Often times we don't even allow ourselves to cry at funerals...Be A Man....Be A Man......<u>that is totally insane</u>. Crying is how we honor our feelings, and how we grieve and heal our great losses. Yet we are often taught to .."just be strong".......and forced to "survive" without this amazing, life affirming...... soothing.... comforting...... nurturing......cleansing....... freeing.....<u>healing</u>..... gift......... of crying........honoring and then releasing deep sadness and grief.....which is about as natural and <u>free</u> as we can get....(along with, of course, crying over great joy.. another part of being truly alive and "thriving").

And we wonder why so many of us men are emotional basket cases. This is usually due to our tenuous hold on our emotions.... our lack of healthy role models and teaching...and the unhealed pain from our childhoods. (What's really scary, is <u>we often have "adult" leaders who are really unhealed little boys, running the show</u>)........ So we strive to be stoic robots.... (yet are allowed to bully with anger...or even act out in rage).... and we wonder why we have racism....and violence against women children, animals, the planet.... and ....war! Speaking of war...the unexpressed trauma, guilt, shame, sadness, fear that many of us vets hold inside from war atrocities we can't share about, for fear of appearing weak, are often the cause of extreme violence, suicidality, addictions and other extreme mental health issues. Crying, leading to sharing openly, would have been a great outlet and healer for a lot of us vets. And the rage, which lives inside us, and causes so much of the horrific atrocities in this world, is most often the result of our untended to tears.

When we <u>tend to our natural inner need to cry</u>, we can feel more at peace with ourselves, and our bodies and minds feel healthier....because we are listening to our inner voice. Many health care practitioners recommend crying to keep our bodies well tuned, and free from dis-ease...emotional, mental, physical. After some great and tender cries....we can feel ....soothing relief.....cleared out....maybe even ready to start the process of eventually letting go of old losses, wounds, and fears that no longer serve us..... We can learn to start making healthy loving decisions... followed by healthy loving action....perhaps by asking ourselves.... "What would love do now?" as our guide. This doesn't mean we won't still grieve some pain and losses, maybe for the rest of our lives. It does, however, mean we can also decide to savor the sweet memories and feelings, heal and appreciate who we are, and what we have now, and in the future.

<u>**My fear of crying governed half of my life**</u>. I know that my absolute terror at being found out to be less than....unworthy..... not smart enough...not good enough.....a liar.... cheat...fraud... weak...a coward.....was the fear that drove so many of my decisions and actions for at least half of my life. Finally in my mid forties, after being suicidal, I got into some serious treatment and recovery and decided that if I was going to choose to live...... I would need to make a life long <u>commitment</u> to learn about real love, and how to really respect, honor and love myself and others, by living in complete integrity, and by facing all of my fears....especially of being vulnerable. So

I started doing some deep grief work, allowing myself to cry, which I hadn't since early childhood (to be a man), along with deep rage work (i.e., yelling at the top of my lungs, beating cushions etc, however being fully committed to not hurting myself or anyone else with it (didn't need more self-inflicted hurt)). As part of my self care routines, I'd set times aside, when I wouldn't be interrupted, and would have some time to rest after (sometimes I would actually feel energized afterwards). Along with meditation, prayer, and journaling, breathing and repeating positive supportive affirmations.... little by little I finally started feeling free of the deep dark block of granite pain in my gut, and started actually liking myself.....and not so afraid of being vulnerable ....actually seeing it as a path to being the man I truly wanted to be. Now, when I see something, or read, or hear a song, or am out it nature and some sensation, or sad memory or thought comes up, and I allow myself to cry....I feel so grateful....so Grate-full.

**As a long time trauma therapist, these days I only work with male trauma clients. And learning how to be gentle and kind...tender-hearted with ourselves, continues to be one of the greatest challenges for most of my clients. Yet, when we are brave enough, to gradually let go of the suit of armor, we start to realize that most of the things we've been looking for outside of ourselves......actually lie inside us.**

**Our unattended to scared little boy will continue to hide inside us, in deep pain.. forever affecting our "adult" lives' feelings and actions.......until we finally begin to listen to and start comforting and healing that most vulnerable part**

**of us. <u>Choosing to become the source of soothing safety, acceptance, comfort and healing love for ourselves, frees us to finally truly be all that we can be.</u>**

Years ago there was an amazing love song I heard....(wish I could remember it and find it)....it basically said....the greatest gift I can give you....is the gift of my tears. Helps me to remember...some of the cherished moments when I have felt closest to another human being were when we held each other and shared our tears. And yet, unfortunately, those moments have been all too few. For me, this is real emotional intimacy... where real trust and safety and love can flourish. As long as, of course, it is part of an ever growing commitment to core ingredients of love......like gentleness, integrity, courage, humility, dependability, kindness, compassion...... And again... some wise one said.... "Each tear is a another drop of healing.... on this life long adventure of healing".

This book.....can be complemented by a companion guide on the essence of healthy crying...which might just be my next one. Or maybe one of you will decide to write it. In the meantime, for more inspiration about the gift of our tears, please see the work of Henri Nouwin, 'Men and Grief', Richard Rohr, 'The Gift of Tears', Dr. Kate Truitt, 'Keep Breathing', and my Dear Friend Dr. Amanda Aminata Kemp with Dr. Sina Smith ('Why is Crying Good'/'Why is Fall the perfect time to grieve', on you tube video, which reminded me of how important crying is for our health...duh... I wouldn't still be here without this amazing gift of my tears)

**Final ..and maybe most important, Initial Guiding Principle...**

6. **Gratitude**- The 12 Step...Attitude of Gratitude....and, perhaps, really **the only thing I have any control over....my Attitude**....to Breathe in Deeply...and Savor all of my Blessings...for which I am sooo grateful........ (Please see **Victor Frankel's beautiful book 'Man's Search for Meaning'**, about his inspiring time in a Nazi prison camp, awaiting imminent death, and yet, choosing an attitude of gratitude, the one thing no one else can control or take from us).

....My Life...........My Love.........My Health.........Incredible Loved Ones In My Life........Being Able to Write this..........The Animals....
The Trees.......And....On....And....On.....And On.....
........And You.... Dear One....For Choosing To Be On This Love Journey.

A wise, wise soul Fran, in one of my mindfulness meditation groups..... after sharing some of the severe health challenges for herself and her partner, told us.... "every morning and night, the most important thing I do for myself....is write the things I'm grateful for." (If you haven't already, please view and listen to a tender, visually beautiful, soothing music video....google..... **'you tube grateful tony moss lyric video'**, (and click on the x in the corner to view on full screen), to see the special version.... moon light rays and water over rocks and comforting words that touch my heart....and hopefully will touch yours too).

# Heart Gratitude

My Heart is Grateful.....for you being You....for Hearing me.........

.....again.......

......in the midst.....

.....of loss......

.....of pain.....

.....of sadness....

.......of grief......

.......and yet.....

......I do Know.....

.....that deep....inside...

....this is all ....a great gift....

......it just sucks some times.....

.....and then.................

...............eventually..........

.....I return home.....

.....to Love.

and re-member.......

......All Is Well.

.....Thank You.

# Grateful

I'm grateful
    For my ever growing
        Conscious contact
That's clearly
    The meat and potatoes
    The pizza and pasta
        Of my life.

With it I have all.
Without it I have nothing.

| | |
|---|---|
| The wind | My work |
| The sky | My song |
| The hawk | My dance |
| The child | My joy |

I have so much love to share
When I'm in conscious contact
With Spirit.

**RS/Summer 02**

# To Be Grateful

Grazie
Gracias
Pilamaya
Wopila

So many ways
to say
Thank You.

So many ways
to Be
Grateful

This racial justice
journey
is fraught full
of unlimited
opportunities
to grow
in love
and wisdom.

This Awakening
With Love
journey
if fraught full
of unlimited
opportunities

to grow
in love
and wisdom.

I am Blessed.

A Thank You...For the Ages.

# Chester Springs Detective

I offered you 2000
  To shoot me in the head
It was something I would welcome,
  Not something I would dread.

The darkness, shame and guilt,
  The sin of "living the lie",
Were all I really needed,
  To convince me I should die.

So I Offered You 2000,
  So my wife and kid would be set,
  (With the life insurance they'd get).
But you told me I needed help.
  The first angel I truly met.

Don't know what I did with the money.
  Probably spent it on qualudes and pot.
But I know one thing Private Eye.
  I'm grateful and thank you a lot.

For after that day I started thinking,
  And eventually decided to live.
I detached from my family and friends,
  And determined what attention to give,

To finding a way to heal,
  From the fear, self-hatred and despair,

By saying no to others,
  So my heart and spirit could repair.

You bought me some precious time
  To learn how to finally love me.
You saw the light in the tunnel,
  That I was too blind to see.

~

I know my loved ones were hurt.
  And that was never my intention.
I was desperate, and at my wit's end.
  So I needed a drastic intervention.

Some dear to me still seem angry.
  And I pray someday they'll understand
That I did what I Needed to do,
  And it was God who had my hand.

I wish them soothing love,
  As I have some sense how they feel.
I wish them compassion and kindness
  So their anger and wounds will heal.

~

It's taken a long time to get solid.
  A process, learning as I go.
I have had lot's of help, long the way,
  From others I didn't even know.

But you Private Eye are the angel,
   Without you, I wouldn't be here.
For I was at the Real Crossroads,
   Between life, and love, and fear.

So I wish I could find you to thank you,
   And show you my feet on the ground.
I guess I'll meet you in heaven,
   Or back here the next time round.

Many years later, I actually did find him to thank him. He
ended up thanking me. He was going through a painful time,
and it made him feel better, more worthwhile, that he had
helped me.

Ft. Pierce
3/05

# PART II

## LOVING SELF-CARE TOOL KIT

*~*

*Loving Ourselves and Others*
*What could be more important than this,*
*as our ultimate life purpose?*

*~*

So before I start sharing some Love Theories and Strategies...
from our Self-Care Skills Tool Kit .....(when I ran the alcohol
and other drug counseling and education program as part of
the Counseling Center at Temple U. in Phily, I had this little red
tool box, that I would point to when a client said they wanted
to learn self care skills........and still talk about that symbolic
self-care tool box to this day)....

........I'd like to share a little poem...which is about..yep, you
guessed it.......and which was also the first poem of my very
first book....which seems like eons ago...and was really only
four years ago...wow...talk about time flying.

# Love

the essence
of love

is deep,
beautiful,
feelings

of unconditional
<u>acceptance</u>
and
appreciation

for
myself
and
for
all
life.

The
<u>interconnected,</u>
harmonious
Oneness

With
creative

universal
energy.

With it
I feel <u>connected</u>,
and
all makes sense.

without it,
disconnected,
and nothing
makes sense.

Hmmm,

think I'll choose
Love.

I am eternally
grateful.

~

So, as we spoke of in my first Eileen story.....the acceptance...
and feeling connected..which helps with feeling more openhearted...and connected to all things.

# A LIFE WORTH LIVING

## The Crystal: A Very Basic Intro To Self-Worth and Love

Many years ago my brother Glenn wrote a wonderful workbook on self-esteem. The image that follows is borrowed from his book with his permission. As soon as I saw it....it so deeply resonated with me.

Mostly because I never, ever ...felt "worthy". As I mentioned in the intro.... I had always felt like a cheat, liar and fraud....and was literally... afraid of my own shadow. Oh and let me add....a "coward." I would run from fights...(would stand up for others and jump into a fight then),...but would only fight if I had to ..to defend myself.

So, I was on this dizzying cycle of always trying to "prove" myself worthwhile, worthy...but mostly just wanting to fit in, and be "seen" as "adequate." And...I never felt like I really fit in...always felt different...and that they would find out who I really was.

Since I never felt "good enough"...it was a never ending battle to just...stay afloat. And can't remember many moments where I actually gave myself any credit. Like I mentioned before, I had a few "successful" moments with sports, when I did something special...yet never, ever gave myself any credit, since I always felt it was just pure luck..(i.e., the winning pass just fell into my hands). It was not until many, many years later, when I had finally <u>chosen</u> to <u>really live</u>...and <u>believe</u> that I was worthy.....

that I finally did say, with almost full conviction.... "yeah that was a great catch!"

The crystal picture which follows reminded me...that everyone is born worthy, and that doesn't have to be proven or earned... it's not about externals....seeking outside approval, goals, grades, awards, material wealth...it just IS.
So we are each a beautiful crystal....that is our essence...our truth...we don't have to do anything to earn it....it just is. And when we get mud on it..which we will from time to time...it still doesn't change anything...we just clean off the mud and get back to honoring our beautiful core crystal self.

The question is, whether I will choose to really **Believe** a paradigm, which basically flies in the face of all the "macho" values which run our world...aggressive, <u>competing</u> to be perfect, #1, better than (no matter who you need to walk over), elitism, superiority, always achieving (not that there's anything wrong with achieving and goals), however..always needing the next goal...<u>to prove I'm worthy</u>...which is a whole other thing...and also....the ultra-elusive butterfly. And the next goal allows me to feel worthy for a minute....and then onto the next goal...and the next goal.....and on and on....And we wonder why we have such a stressful multi-tasking world. Of course we <u>naturally</u> want to keep "growing", and becoming better versions of ourselves....like learning how to improve on some skill...etc...yet ...... whether we do or not.....we ....still...are..... worthy....worthwhile....and damn it.......
fully.....ADEQUATE.....ACCEPTABLE.................

....<u>SACRED</u>....as in .... "All Life Is Sacred"...(thus the proposal later on...please be clear..this is not about religion...as some religions teach beautiful lessons of love....and the "sacred"....and some don't...and all too often the messages are bastardized to serve those in power)...so Sacred meaning <u>important, valuable, precious (like a rare jewel), worthy of Love, dignity, respect, wonder and awe.......and that All Life is Sacred...and I'm no better no worse than that insect, that tree, that plant, that child, that woman..or that other man.....that All Life is Sacred.</u> And Love thy neighbor....as thyself ... <u>As you love yourself</u>...(clearly not about selfish, self-centered ego maniacal...that ain't love)... however the original beautiful message of love.. and all life is sacred, worthwhile worthy....is soooo <u>lost</u> in the translation. And we wonder why...we all feel soooo lost in a world so alienated from ....Love.

Imagine how different the world would be ..if that was the core value, the core belief, the core mission of schools, churches, and families.....teaching this value....and the core principle behind the decisions of our governments, our military, our police forces, our corporations, prisons, banks ...and that our "leaders"...had "Love and their guiding principles...and related values like....compassion, and honesty, and courage and humility and equity....that they held themselves..... and we held them and ourselves accountable to......whew....how different our world would be. I will repeat this ....as I believe it bares repeating.

# Worth

Each of us is born worthy.
     That worth lives inside us.

It's who we are.

     If we're not taught it,
It's up to us to choose it.
     This road ain't easy.

Self-Worth
The Core Self
Sacred

The Beautiful Crystal
is the image
of the
core self,

sacred...

worthwhile,
worthy of love,
valuable,
precious,
born this way.

Doesn't have to be **earned...**

This is our essence.....

rather than externals ....
like goals,
achievement,
others' approval,
wealth,
being #1,
"success."

There may be
mud on the crystal....
but when I clean it off.....
the crystal remains....
worthwhile
beautiful,
worthy of love.

Teaching our parents
that This
is the most important message
to give their young ones....
"I love you unconditionally....
and no matter what you do or accomplish,
that's all gravy.......
I love you for Being Alive

I love you for Being You"

This is why so many
are suicidal,
because they truly believe
they can never do enough

or Be enough
to earn
their parents love.

And if worth
is judged
by color of skin,
race,
nationality,
gender,
sexual orientation,
disability,
economic status,
and other considerations......
this is a huge obstacle
to ever feeling
fully acceptable
and worthwhile.

I choose
to Believe
in my core worth......
and all others'...
and all life's core worth....
all life is sacred....
and we are all connected,

and all one....

let it be so....

This
is what I choose
to believe.

Hope you do...too.

If this is what we taught and lived by.....our parents, teachers, churches, police, military, bosses....presidents....government.... all of our institutions....all of us....

....racism...and the white supremacy culture which breeds it... and all the other "isms'....would be a dead issue.

# SELF WORTH

## Rather than external e.g. goals others approval, wealth, being

The Core Self

Externals

Externals

Core Worth
(Essential, Spiritual Self)

# Healthy Values Intro

.......which brings us to a sampling of "<u>healthy</u>" <u>values </u>to choose to live by...in support of our core worth...(healthy... meaning they support us in <u>continually growing into better and better versions of our most loving selves</u>).............. and again...what we "need" to be teaching and modeling for our young ones....and <u>the most important mission</u> and <u>core function</u> of our families, schools, churches, government, businesses, ... all our "institutions".... is to provide a foundation which reinforces these healthy core values.........(please see the "All Life is Sacred" Proposal later on).....

....and the accomplishments, accumulations...etc., etc... are all gravy.....but not the determinant of our worth, happiness, success, serenity, etc......

The following was used as part of a keynote presentation on "Men and Multicultural Counseling". The belief is that, as we support our boys and men, and all of us, to embrace and live by our most healthy human values, racism will eventually die out.

# Values

It's About Values
And Taking A Stand

This being human,
Always a <u>choice</u>.
When to take a stand,
and lend our voice.

<u>Knowing</u> our values
Being firm and clear,
Always a choice,
between love and fear.

So let's see now....

"<u>Unhealthy</u>",
   <u>traditional,</u>
<u>masculine,</u>
   <u>values;</u>

competition
      elitism
entitlement
      superiority

power
    wealth
success
    control

Or,

<u>"Healthy",</u>
    <u>traditional,</u>
<u>feminine,</u>
    <u>(and "healthy",</u>
<u>male,</u>
    <u>values:</u>

cooperation
    sharing
generosity
    consideration
nurturance
    kindness
support
    encouragement

And,

"Healthy",
     traditional
human,
     values:

integrity
     dependability
courage
     humility
gentleness
     strength
service
     respect
equity
     patience
compassion.


Alright now...
hope that helps you some
always important to figure
where we're coming from.

# Moral Inventory and Valuing Process

The following inventory was developed by my brother Glenn and adapted by me with his permission. Glenn is a caring teacher and writer about resilience and healing from trauma - (please check out his books and workbooks.) The idea here is to take a fair and non-critical look at our character strengths / values, first looking at how we treat ourselves, and then how we treat others. The number 1-10 serves as a guide to what improvements we may wish to make. In general, the valuing process is as follows:

Clarifying and understanding, the meaning and implications of each value.

Choosing, after carefully considering alternatives and consequences of living each value.

Taking action, which consistently reflects chosen values.


(Two other versions of this inventory (for leaders and institutions) appear as part of the All Life is Sacred Proposal, later on in this book).

# The Fearless, Searching, Kind Moral Inventory*

## No person can be truly at peace with himself if he does not live up to his moral capacity - Norman Cousins**

| Character Strength | Rate Yourself from 1-10. 10 means you are living this strength as well as a person can. | | Describe a time in the past when you demonstrated this strength | | Describe what you could do to demonstrate this strength better and more often. | |
|---|---|---|---|---|---|---|
| | Self | Others | Self | Others | Self | Others |
| Courage means persisting in doing the right thing despite the pressure to do otherwise. | | | | | | |
| Honesty means you speak only the truth, always. No "white lies," half-truths (truth can be tactful and kind), cheating or stealing. | | | | | | |
| Integrity means your behaviors match your values and that you show your sincere, authentic self without pretense. | | | | | | |
| Respect means you honor people and treat them as worthwhile; are civil and courteous. | | | | | | |
| Fairness means you play by the rules, do not take dishonorable advantage of others, and treat others impartially. | | | | | | |
| Loyalty, faithfulness, and trustworthiness means you keep commitments and confidences, don't speak ill of others behind their backs; reliable. | | | | | | |
| Responsible means able and willing to respond to valid needs and duties; dependable; protects self and others. | | | | | | |
| Kind, caring means you are concerned for the welfare of others, desire to help and support their growth; considerate, generous, tenderhearted. | | | | | | |
| Sexual integrity means sexual expression is used in the context of love and concern for the other, and never used in a selfish or exploitive way. | | | | | | |
| Tolerant means you are patient with differences and imperfections of others; forgiving | | | | | | |

*Reprinted with permission from Schiraldi, G. R. (2011), *The Complete Guide to Resilience: Why It Matters; How to Build and Maintain It*. Ashburn, VA: Resilience Training International. © 2011 Glenn R. Schiraldi, Ph.D.

# Values Meditation and Prayer

May we each continually choose to live by our most beautiful loving values.

May we always to our best "to listen to that little, still voice of truth inside, which gently guides us home again, to re-member, to re-connect with, our grandest version of our greatest vision of who we truly are."

~

**(With deep appreciation to Neale Donald Walsch and his 'Conversations With God' books).**
**Neale teaches us, that when we are facing a quandary, dilemma, painful, or scary decision, etc...we have simply to quite our minds..and ask ourselves the simple (yet likely the greatest) question we can ever ask ourselves.....**
**"*What would love do now?*".... "*What would be the most loving thing I can do for myself?*"**
**That little voice of truth will always provide the answer.... we will know it is true....however we might not want to hear it...because the loving path is not always the easiest...and takes lots of courage. Yet, we can be assured, it will always end up being in our best interest.**
**And in the best interest of the others...even though they will often not like it because they are not getting their way. However, it will also end up being in their best interest too.**

*(Another very important little book 'The Four Agreements' by DonMiguel Ruiz, where he shares four important agreements to make with ourselves to live happy, healthy lives. The first and most essential is..To Be Impeccable With Our Word, which I see as The core ingredient of Love.)*

~

*The Greatest Power in the Universe*
*Is LOVE*
*With it...All things are possible*
*Without it......good luck.*

~

# Healing Love

## Healing Love

I Have
unlimited love

I Am
Unlimited Love

I Share
unlimited love

I Have
unlimited
possibilities
with this
truth

My Creativity
is limitless
with this
truth

THIS
IS
MY
FREE,
COURAGEOUS,

COMPASSIONATE,
CHOICE

TO LIVE
IN LOVE.

When I am
bathed
in love,
I see
white supremacy
for what
it is.....
a lie
of fear.

It's got to start
with the truth.

We don't have
a common story,
a common truth
of our history.

Very hard
to heal
a lie,
an open
wound
that's still
infected.

Hard
to love
a lie.

However,
I can find it
in me....
ever so deep....
to love
the liar......
whew....
now that's
Big Love.

For the liar
is in me,
I'm no better
no worse.
So compassion
is the deal,
not judgment....
compassion
for me,
compassion
for the other,
compassion
for all things..
especially since

all living things
are sacred.

When I speak truth
with love,
all things
are possible,
my creativity
can flourish.

With this
most powerful
force,
all things
can be healed.

Without it,
there are
limited possibilities.
competition and fear
are very limited
indeed.

Being humble.....
and vulnerable.....
wo....
that really hits it.

Full on,
full in,
fully myself,

nothing
held back,
all in.

Grounded
in love,
I am aware,
fully conscious
of me
and all
around me,
so I see
possibilities,
and I see
roadblocks

Love is
the miraculous
antidote
for hatred,
and fear.

I am love
.....we all are

I am love
**.....we all are.**

# Wholistic Health Wheel

This was the model that was taught to me by my mentor Marv Levy, who threatened to put his big...(he was a big man) size 13 foot up my butt, if I threatened to quit ...my doctoral program, because of my fear of not being able to handle the academics. We used it as a foundation for training the counselors, teachers and students in the alcohol and other drug prevention program. The teachers were urged to use it for their lesson plans, addressing each of the effective/affective learning domains (mental, emotional, physical, social, spiritual).(Spiritual is for you to determine...for me it's anyway that helps me feel most alive and lovingly connected to the universe and my most pure self.. can be Nature, Higher Power...prayer, ceremony, depends on the individual...more recently, I call "her" Mother Love Creator and Universal Love, Universal One, and each morning I sit at an altar I created with candles, sage, sweet grass, symbols of love, and "call in" my ancestors for reminders of who I am and why I am here and to breathe and give gratitude.). The affective domain is a huge one for me....especially when I was younger...(however still is mostly true).......because if something didn't touch me emotionally....it was much more likely that it wouldn't resonate with me...and that I wouldn't remember it. So it stood to reason then, that this was a powerful foundation for considering change....values...

........healthy living strategies. The idea being....if I wasn't feeling healthy or happy in one domain...it was likely, that the other domains were also being affected..and vice versa....and were each needing some tending to. If I was feeling emotionally upset about something….it could very easily effect my mental, physical, social, spiritual capacity etc.

A good blueprint to refer back to ….when I was feeling off kilter.

And the second wheel below...the "pie of life wheel"….a typical 24 hour day (although one sharp client observed the numbers added up to more than 24 hours (math was always my greatest challenge in school). So how does my "normal" day ideally (not perfectly) reflect the holistic health wheel. Do I schedule, and do my best to have balance in my days ..ie., time for exercise, calling a friend to say hi, doing something creative, time for eating "mindfully" (more a little later), enough time for good sleep etc..

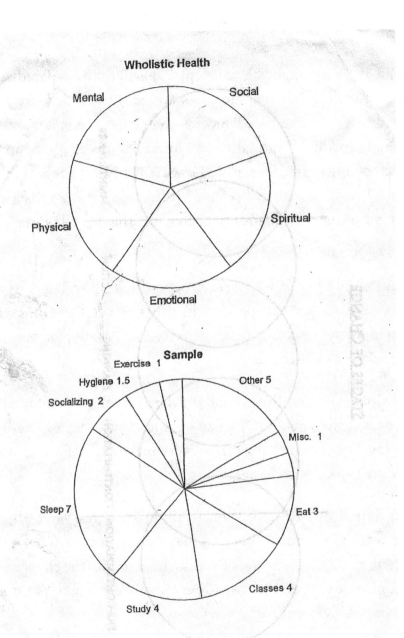

**Wholistic Health**

Mental

Social

Physical

Spiritual

Emotional

**Sample**

Exercise 1

Hygiene 1.5

Socializing 2

Other 5

Misc. 1

Sleep 7

Eat 3

Study 4

Classes 4

# Readiness for Change

This is a very important concept as part of our preparedness for embarking on specific goals and strategies. If we're not ready... it's not likely we'll meet with much success. Readiness is an individual thing....different for each individual. It's up to each of us to decide when, and if we're ready. If I keep landing back in jail....it's likely because I still haven't made a decision / commitment to change the behaviors that keep landing me there.

And seeing the process as a process...that often happens in steps...or stages, can be very helpful for keeping things in perspective, and not getting us too frustrated or feeling hopeless, or self-critical.

Two researchers, Prochaska and DeClemente, developed a process called Stages Of Change, initially to address healing from addictions (or habits), however can be helpful for whatever we are working to change.

It's important to note, this is about "progress, not about perfection" (from 12 Step), as many changes take time, and, often, re-strategizing and on and on to maintain the change we seek (so clearly persistence and perseverance, being committed, yet not self-critical are key elements).

So the basic elements...can be visualized as 5 inter-connected circles...starting with "pre-contemplation (we're not thinking about the change), "contemplation" (we're thinking about it), "planning" (we start coming up with strategies), "action" (we start putting the plan into action), and "maintaining" (keeping it going). And we may likely, go back and forth among the different stages, as we continue improving our efforts. (Prochaska, J.O., DiClemente, C.C., The Transtheoretical Model (2005), Handbook of Psychotherapy Integration, Oxford, NY.)

<u>This Healing Path</u>.....<u>is ongoing</u>....til our last breath....and then some.

Change.....Growth......Stillness...

....Solid....Wavering.....Inter-Connected.....

..........With All Life....With All Things.....

One of my Great Teachers Aminata....Dr. Amanda Kemp (for a pod cast interview with her, please see my web site)...reminding me of a very important lesson.....in the midst of some, deep deep grief work.......

I started feeling very very vulnerable....given a flash of old old guilt and shame over hurting someone long ago.....in this life... and likely in another life.....I thought I had healed that and let it go.....made amends....committed to never repeating that behavior......honored that....
..........and yet....still....the flash of guilt and shame....hit me.....I think it was triggered from a passage in a book I was reading.... (sometimes it can come from a scene in a movie, or a song.... or ...the wind......lots of different sources////triggers.......

anyway.......she reminded me....this kind of deep pain, sensitivity....opening old wounds...traumas....etc....

can be a Beautiful......

Opportunity

For Deeper

Healing

LOVE............

..................FORGIVNESS..............

................................................PEACE........................

..............................................................JOY..............

A Reassuring Reminder from the Ancestors.........

"We're All OK!!"

"ALL IS WELL"

A call for........

RELEASING..........

.............................FREEING.......

ALL That is NOT....

<u>.My Most Pure Loving Self</u>.

All Is Well.

I Am Love.

The Ancestors …..The Gentle Wind Spirits …..

…..........And The POWERFUL Wind Spirits......

Always reminding me............

"Re-member....Who You Are"

We Are With You.......In You.....Always With You........

…......YOU …......ARE........LOVE.........

…....................................................ALL IS WELL.

Breathing In Love. To Me.

Breathing Out Love...To All.

A Word of Caution- The following tool....called The Suicide / Self Care Contract.....can be a challenging one, since it does talk about suicidality. If you are on the fence with suicidality...you might want to pass on using this next tool, at least for the time being.

If you are actively suicidal ....either thinking about it, or planning it, or making gestures...I would highly encourage you either call 911, or go to the nearest emergency room, if it may be imminent, and if not, then please start looking for a good therapist...someone who you can build trust with, tell everything to, and who can support you in using some of the following tools to get the most benefit out of them. This work is too difficult to do alone. We all need and deserve support. Many therapists can be found on Google, and through Psychology Today (I suggest you have a phone consult, whenever possible, to screen them to get a feel for if you might feel safe and comfortable with them.)

And NOW....a powerful, powerful self-care tool:

# The Suicide / Self-Care Contract

**<u>(And a few other related self-care tools that are all very powerful... if we choose to own them and use them for our LOVE). Again, each of these, has so helped me...and many, many others to have the lives they really wanted.</u>**

So this is **The** instrument...**The** agreement....**The** contract.... **The** Commitment....that saved my life. Without it...I wouldn't still be here writing this book about love. I'm clear about that.

So the contract is about 1. <u>making a life long commitment to stop hurting myself and/or others...in all the ways I do it... mentally, emotionally, physically, socially, spiritually</u>.... 'cause I'm slick ...so I can be muckin myself over.....and think I'm takin care of myself...and only half steppin....or even ..settin myself up for disaster...or at least...a serious hurtin. And 2. <u>to start making a life-long commitment to do all I can to take loving care of myself so I can have the happiest, healthiest life, which we each so deserve, emotionally, mentally, socially, spiritually, physically....the ultimate full monte.</u>

So this is about takin some serious inventory...and not givin myself any outs. Let's please be clear...I'm not sayin to further beat myself up. I am sayin to stop hurtin myself, and start <u>holdin myself accountable</u>....fully, all in...**100% accountable... for every thought word and action.** And if they are congruent with my core values........great..ya hoo....I'm good. If they are not....no big drama...no big hoopydoo....just pick myself up, dust myself off....figure out how I ..once again..(cause it's usually not the first time), set myself up to the same ol same ol....come up with a better strategy, and put it into motion, so I can start feeling good about myself again. That's it...it's not real complicated. However, it is the full monte. If I want to have a great life like I was put here for...I need to stop screwin myself over.

And the smart ones will say...oh crap this contract is serious... there's no more outs / excuses for me etc...yep...and yep. However...you're also smart enough to see...that this is also a ticket to freedom...from all the things that keep sabotaging our healthiest happiest lives.

Its' called "suicide"/self-care...because while many of you may not be actively suicidal...if we're not committed to self-care and learning how to love ourselves and fully live ....and we keep screwin ourselves over ...again and again.....then we may not be puttin a gun to our head..but we might just as well.. to save ourselves the on- going trauma / misery...over and over again....our systems can only take so much before....the slow, excruciating episodes....become habitual....which begets <u>disease</u>........and on and on......and before we know it.... poof....we're gone. That may seem overly simplistic...however......ah..well... nuff said. We're either committed to our optimal self care... Love...or we're not. If we're half in and half out...then that's the results we get.

And the word...<u>accidentally</u>...wo....that definitely takes care of all my outs. The idea is..if I leave this computer right now, and walk downstairs and trip and break my leg..was it an <u>accident</u>?

I would, respectfully say....if I got my head out of my butt, and was paying attention to every step I was takin...and not rushing or multitasking etc.....i clearly wouldn't have had the "accident". I firmly believe that "all" accidents can be prevented. "Oh yeah?"...I hear you sayin... "what if I'm stopped at a light and this wack job comes up behind me?".....well then....as my ex-traffic cop trainer (for my safe driving course to get my speeding ticket points reduced) told us....when you get in that death trap you had best be concentrating on one thing........ driving...always checking rearview/sideview mirrors, and **not**....I repeat **not**...fiddlin with the radio, or smart phone..ear phones (hands free, even)...or whatever else...because a split second is all it takes. My therapists always taught be to say the Suicide / Self – Care Contract before I put the key in the ignition.

And the rest of the contract is pretty self explanatory. If I hurt others...it will hurt me....if I keep doin the same ol same ol, and not seeing set ups and warning signs........talk about accidents waiting to happen.......

....and listening to the little voice of truth and love inside, and what's in our best interest.....................

.........and to not live with this self care commitment, doesn't make much sense....and really...when we boil it all down...... is ...flat out...crazy.

But it's definitely our CHOICE.

# The (Suicide) / Self-Care Contract

**I will not accidentally or intentionally, hurt, harm or kill myself.**

**I will not accidentally or intentionally hurt, harm or kill anyone else.**

**I will not accidentally or intentionally set myself up.**

**I will not accidentally or intentionally go crazy.**

**I will stay fully present, in this moment, listening to my heart and my instincts.**


It is most helpful to say this contract out loud in the mirror when first making the commitment (feeling the strength and conviction and implications). And **before doing rage work**, or anything where we might hurt or injure ourselves. And making lists of all the ways we hurt ourselves and/or others, emotionally, mentally, physically, spiritually, socially, with specific and reasonable strategies and time lines to address the way we set ourselves up to hurt ourselves, and/or others.

~

# Fear Bubble-up

This is another very basic, and hugely helpful strategy to help sort through and empower ourselves with the Fear/s that are holding us back.

Suggest start with putting categories listed horizontally across page, if have the space. Then picking one fear to start...then exaggerate ..i.e., continue to ask, what might happen next, and then what.. etc., then other related feelings, then reality check ie. What's the likelihood that might happen, then specific strategies, obstacles to each, and strategies for those, and realistic time line for each.

Fears  Exaggerate Fears  Other feelings  Reality Check

Strategies        Obstacles        Time line

# Goals / Strategies

A simple, effective tool for clarifying our goals and strategies, and to keep us on tract.

1. Write overall general goal for your relationship with core issue (whatever you choose it to be), moving forward.

2. List obstacles / roadblocks, set-ups which prevent success with overall goal.

3. List <u>specific</u> and <u>realistic</u> strategies for being successful with overall goal. (If they're not specific and realistic, given what we know of ourselves, they won't work.)

4. Do the same with more specific goals.

~

# Anger / Rage Work

Doing anger and rage work are important gifts to give ourselves and our loved ones, as it frees us from adding to pent up frustrations, which can easily lead to hurtful behavior towards ourselves or others.

It is essential to always remind ourselves of our **commitment to do no harm to ourselves or others, when we decide to do our anger/rage work** (rage is simply the more extreme version of anger, left unattended). Either way, it is important to be certain, that being <u>**"out of control" is never an option, so if we have doubts about our ability to honor our commitment to ourselves to do no harm, then we should practice by doing less threatening versions,**</u> such as journaling, listing things we're angry at, speaking them out loud etc. It is also important to be specific about verbal or violent behavior which we commit to avoiding. When coaching / supporting another, this can be so helpful, to voice out loud those behaviors which we agree are not acceptable. We can practice by starting out with verbalizing who or what we are angry at, and why. If that expressing, and resulting exploration of the feelings, doesn't seem to be sufficient, then rage work may be the next option. (If the coach / support person is one of the sources of the rage, it is important to first determine whether it is a good idea to be present, both to not stifle the other, and because of the pain of hearing it).

Children can be especially receptive to this type of emotional work, as it allows them to yell, be physical, and not feel censored.

It is often much more difficult for adults, since we have had many more years of censorship with our emotions.

Rage work is a great way to get to the heart of what is ailing us (always preceded by a re-commitment to the self-care contract). 1. We may then prepare by writing down some key words memories, phrases, etc, that trigger our anger, and perhaps place them around a stick figure picture which represents who or what we are angry at. (coaches can support / prime the pump, by encouraging the other to confront the bully or other source of anger) 2. Then we place the picture on a pillow or bean bag chair, kneel on another pillow and start talking to the picture, and eventually yelling at the top of lungs at whoever or whatever we are angry at, and what we are at, and why, 3. while simultaneously hitting the pillow with a plastic wiffle ball bat, until we feel like we have gotten all the anger feelings out. (Tears may flow along with the rage, which is great, because it means we are getting to the core hurt underneath the anger). Usually after about 5 or 10 minutes of yelling, and hitting, we are beat, and then need to rest, and tend to our raw feelings. If it is done right, we are usually exhausted, feeling vulnerable, and yet, with a wonderfully empowering feeling of freedom from the chains that have been binding us. Some hints: a. choose a space where you don't have to worry about noise disturbing others (if have close neighbors, you can alert them you are doing therapy work, and b. you can yell into a pillow, and it does a great job of muffling the sound. Also yelling in the woods, or by the ocean are other great venues.

Anger / rage work, if done with care, and respect for self, and other, is an absolutely effective way of freeing ourselves from the toxic poison that left unattended, can lead to harmful results.

The family that rages together, flourishes, and loves together.

(**Of course this requires being done with utmost respect, care and safety**).

# Non Violent Communication (NVC)

This is a wonderful approach to deeper healing and connecting with ourselves and others. It teaches us how to communicate with ourselves and others with clarity, compassion, empathy. NVC was developed by Marshall Rosenberg, and offered in his many inspiring books and training programs on Non Violent Communication. It was taught to me by my dear friend Eliane Guerin. This is a very brief description of the NVC process for self-care. (Please consider some of Marshall's books and attending some training programs).

There are four basic questions, which I have used over and over with myself (and many of my clients), primarily for the purpose of giving self-empathy and compassion, honoring my _feelings_.. and meeting my own _needs_. Other related questions can be used to offer compassion and empathy to others, in our efforts to better connect in healthy ways and resolve conflicts.

_First_ I ask myself, what happened, what are the objective facts of what occurred (without judgment or criticism).

_Next_, I ask myself, what were the _feelings_ that came up for me, and still might be feeling i.e., am I angry, sad, scared, frustrated etc.

_Then_, what I am _needing_ to help me feel better about the situation..ie., am (or was I) needing ...appreciation, respect, safety, acceptance, understanding..etc.

And finally...what I can <u>request of myself</u> now, to meet the un-met needs that led to the feelings...ie., say to say to myself..." whew that was rough...I appreciate you, I respect you, I accept you, I will keep you safe, etc.,"

I have found repeatedly, when I use this process for me....it always helps to de-escalate my need to be understood, or have the other change...I may even decide that I don't feel the need to address them at all....since I have met my own needs.

The process goes on to elaborate with how to connect better with others...however, since most of us have not learned how to be compassionate and gentle with ourselves, this, to me, is the most essential starting point. And likely, getting better at hearing others and bridging the gap can follow.

When I used to be in a particularly stressful work setting, I would carry a little pad and paper, and if I felt myself getting upset by some one else's behavior...I would pull out my pad and pencil and breathe, and write answers to the four questions... and more often than not...it diffused the situation...because I took care of my feelings and needs. I felt heard and respected.

# Healthy Relationships With Others.....

I have found that healthy relationships with others, are most often, a reflection of my healthy relationship.... with ...guess....who?

Yep....I think by now you've got it....likely had it...way before this book. Either way.....I know ..one thing for absolute sure certainty...when I am doing a good job of Being loving........ gentle...kind...compassionate....respectful....appreciative........... accepting........with me.....
....my relationships with others....are most often a reflection of those same values...and behaviors.

And looking for others to do it for me....is not a good strategy for my self care.

Please know....(as my ex-father in law once said "They never said it would be easy."). Healthy relationships with ourselves and others are "the gifts of life" (as a great teacher Vince DiPasaquale, wisely shares in his beautiful booklet..'Healthy Relationships, The Gift Of Life'). However, they can also provide some of the most challenging "growth opportunities" ..ever imagined. That's why knowing and having love as our guiding principle... is ...essential.

~

As wise ones have said.... "The perfect relationship does exist.....
guess who it's with?"....

~

# Marriage Prayer

What follows is a Marriage Prayer. A young daughter of a friend in treatment with me, asked if I would go with her to the ocean to bare witness to her sacred ceremony. She told me she was tired of waiting for her boyfriend...or anyone else....she was finally going to commit to ...Herself. I was, and still am ..in awe of her wisdom, courage, and ...Love for Herself. What a great inspiration. I used it for Eileen and me, and ..so many clients have found it helpful.

# Marriage Prayer

**Given that I am the only person I will be with 24-7 for the rest of my life...**

**I Choose:**

**To Love, Honor, and Cherish Myself Exactly As I Am.**

**To Accept, Acknowledge, and Respect Myself**

**To Be My Own Best Friend For The Rest of My Life.**

**To Always Take Care of Myself**

**To Always Do My Best To Keep Growing With Love, and Sharing That Love With Others.**

# Introduction to Mindfulness Meditation

Mindfulness Meditation, developed by Dr.Jon Kabot-Zinn, is the beautiful, simple practice of continually returning to the breath to help us to be fully present, to every thought, feeling, sound and bodily sensation, to everything within and without, without being swept away by any of it. So it is about clearing, grounding ourselves to be fully alive. Breathing is a celebration of our lives – without it, we cease to exist. This practice is a powerful self-care tool which can serve to improve our clarity, and alertness and provide a sense of calm and well-being. Medical Science continues to demonstrate that a regular practice of Mindfulness Meditation can also help to provide significant relief for stress related illness/dis-ease, and psychological and emotional distress.

Two examples of how to conceive of the approach of Mindfulness may be helpful:

1. Imagine entering into an empty theater all alone, sitting with a projector behind us projecting our lives up on the screen, our actions and behaviors, our thoughts, feelings, sounds, sensations, as we are watching our lives go before us, objectively, without any judgments or criticism, just objectively observing. "Oh that's interesting, there's me having those thoughts, and those feelings, very interesting.

2. Imagine sitting by the edge of a stream, looking at a large, round bolder in the middle of the stream, very calming.

And then we notice many leaves and twigs floating by. The leaves and twigs are like the thoughts and feelings and sensations and sounds. We notice each, breathe and return to the calm of the boulder, and don't get swept along with the thoughts, feelings, sounds or sensations.

The power and beauty of this practice, this discipline is that we can train ourselves to have confidence that we are not the victims of our thoughts, feelings, sounds and sensations, and certainly not controlled by them or anybody, or anything outside of ourselves. WE are the source of calm and comfort and safety, deep inside.

References:

Full Catastrophe Living, by Jon Kabat-Zinn, MD
The Mindful Brain by Dan Siegel, MD
(Other related books by Kabat-Zinn and Siegel)
Mindfulness & Acceptance in Multicultural Competency by Akihiko Masuda, PhD

CDs/Guided Meditation:

Breathing (CD), by Andrew Weil, MD
Mindfulness For Beginners (CD), Kabat-Zinn
Meditation for Optimum Health (CD), Weil (and Kabat-Zinn)
Relieve Stress (CD), Belleruth Naparstek, (Health Journeys)
Healthful Sleep (CD), Naparstek
Depression (CD), Naparstek
Healing From Trauma (CD), Naparstek

# 4 Step Basic Mindfulness Meditation

We start by welcoming each breath, breathing in and breathing out, noticing the rhythm, flow, depth, temperature of the breath, as we begin this beautiful, simple practice, this loving gift of remembering, who we really are, and of reconnecting with our essential nature of health and wholeness, and love. Just noticing the rhythm, not trying to control it. Through this nurturing discipline of breathing, we recreate a sacred space for ourselves in our world.

1. We notice the <u>thoughts</u>, running through our mind, as they always do, (releasing any judgment or criticism). We welcome, acknowledge and honor each thought, by labeling it "thinking" or "thought", and then use each as a gentle reminder to return home to the breath, the place of safety and quiet and stillness, deep inside. We may need to repeat this many times in the beginning, as we are so used to letting our thoughts, feelings and sensations run us.

2. Next we notice, acknowledge and honor each <u>feeling</u> (again releasing any judgment), label each "feeling", or "emotion", and returning home to breath.

3. We then notice any <u>sounds</u>, acknowledge each, label each "sound", and use each as a gentle reminder to return home to breath.

4. And finally we do a full <u>body scan</u>, noticing all sensations (tiredness, soreness tenderness, tenseness), breathing in loving kindness to each part of our body, tending to each sensation with the breath, starting with each toe, tops of our feet, skin, bones, bottom of our feet, arch, heel, ankle, the whole foot, then, calves, thighs, all the organs in the lower torso, base of our spinal column, each vertebrae, one into the other, the muscles and tendons as we move up the spinal column to mid, and then upper back, around to the front torso, lungs and diaphragm, heart beating, pumping blood and oxygen to every artery and vein, down to the toes, up around to our finger tips then up to our brains, our upper arms, forearms, wrists, hand, each finger, palms and tops of hands, shoulders, neck, muscles and tendons, perhaps gently rolling the neck and shoulders as we breath/ massage each part, the skull, hair connected to scalp, each sensation, vibrations, energy, chin, jaw, loosening, breathing, lips, each tooth, tongue, sinuses, eyes and eye sockets, temples and forehead, breathing in soothing and comforting all the brain stuff inside our brain that works so hard all day, breathing out and releasing any worries or thoughts, just for this moment, no where to go nothing to do, but be here now, in this precious moment.

<u>Additional helpful mindfulness related practices</u>:

Noticing the rhythm of the breathing, without trying to control or alter, just noticing, the rhythm. Like the rhythms of the ocean, the waves rolling in and out, the ins and outs of our lives.

Noticing that each breath has a beginning, middle and end, just like each thought, feeling, sound, sensation, each life, beginning, middle and end.

Noticing in between each in breath and out breath, that place of stillness and quiet, deep inside. And between each out breath and each in breath, that place of stillness and quiet deep inside.

<u>4 Step Metta Loving Kindness Practice</u>:

We breathe and feel and envision ourselves filled with and enveloped and surrounded by loving kindness, and then imagine sending that loving energy to those around us, then to our loved ones, and then to all beings everywhere, a circle of ever increasing light and love touching all life everywhere.

We can insert loving kindness affirmations such as peace, love, safety, health, happiness, which ever touch us in the moment, and especially for any special intentions for ourselves and others.

For example:

May I be Healthy and Happy
May all here be Healthy and Happy
May all my Loved Ones be healthy and Happy
May all Beings everywhere be Healthy and Happy

With gentleness and kindness to all.
The Divine in Me Bows to the Divine in You.
Namaste.

# Conscious Eating

We invite you to take several minutes
to practice conscious eating.

You may find the following suggestions helpful.

Look at the color of the food.
Take a deep breath and smell its aroma.
Relax your body, and take a small bite of food.
Chew slowly, staying conscious of the flavor and aroma.
After swallowing, take one deep breath
before taking another bite.
Take a moment to give thanks for the
nourishment this food provides.
Consider how pleasurable it might be
to eat most meals in this way.

# Affirmations

Affirmations are a tool for correction our old misperceptions about ourselves. We replace the old, erroneous messages in our lives with positive, truthful ones These new messages call our attention to the choices we make in our lives - minute by minute, day by day - as we feel our own feelings and allow our own experiences. We can restate them to fit our own unique situations. One way I have found to be helpful...is breathing in the affirmations....and slowly breathing out and saying something like... "I release all worry and fear."

1 I am loving and lovable.

2. I set limits and make them clear.

3. I am a worthwhile person.

4. I allow myself to be relaxed and enjoy life.

5. I am caring and competent.

6. I feel serene and peaceful.

7. I feel calm and clear-headed.

8. Confrontation is affirming my caring
for others in a positive way.

9. I can be forgiving and forgiven.

10. I am intelligent.

11. I can ask questions without guilt or fear.

12. I am responsible for making my own decisions.

13. I am strong.

14. My spiritual and physical existence is who I am, and not dependent on any one person's approval.

15. I am whole in and of myself.

Everything we've explored up until now...has been in preparation for what follows....**The All Life is Sacred Proposal**...which is filled with the **Essential Ingredients** for a Happy... Healthy..... Love filled life.....
for ourselves....our country....our planet.....all offered here for you to savor.

I have presented it in all of my books...because I see it as a gift of Loving Life for All Of Us.

~

This proposal is offered, with hope that all those in power (including you and me), will consider going back to the beginning, to boldly, lovingly, recreate a new vision for ourselves and each other. A Loving Vision of the Sacred... for Healing America...and our world. I offer you this, with hope and faith in our individual and collective commitment to living our lives with full love....Being all we truly can be.

### ALL LIFE IS SACRED

*A Loving Blueprint*
*For Healing America*

*"I am poor and naked, but I am the chief of the nation. We do not want riches, but we do want to teach our children well. Riches would do us no good. We could not take them with*

*us to the other world. We do not want riches. We want peace and love"*

**-Red Cloud (Makhipiya)**
**(late 19 century) Lakota Chief**

# Introduction: The Original Core Values

To Review:......While our Constitution espoused positive sounding values of liberty and justice for "All The People"... Women and Native People were excluded from the document, and African American males were counted as $3/5^{th}$ of a person. Beautiful values and guiding principles of Love - honesty, fairness, kindness, compassion, generosity, respect.... were largely forgotten in the desperate quest for power, wealth and domination.

So in actuality, at it's core, the U.S.'s founding values were more indicative of fear, greed, hatred, material wealth, power and control, which further devolved to elitism, entitlement, superiority. "Success", was equated to competing to be #1, at all costs, no matter who we need to walk over to get there. Those initial values were derived by the misguided principles of "doctrine of discovery" by "god's anointed ones", justifying "manifest destiny". Those principles resulted in the genocide of the Indigenous People, the original inhabitants and stewards of the land, and the horrific inter-generational treatment of enslaved Africans upon whose backs our country's economy was largely built. Additionally, the careless slaughter of the animals and desecration of the land....all for the use of those in power.

The aforementioned paved the way for protecting those in power by establishing and justifying institutional core values of racism, sexism, homophobia, classism, xenophobia, ableism, ageism and on and on. So yes, we have many blessings, and of course, we also have many severe problems. So that's the quick and very dirty, explanation for the state of affairs we find ourselves in.

Now.....what do we do about it?

## Choosing New Core Values To Live By:

## All Life Is Sacred

Again, as I see it...the answer is really quite simple....and yet.... profoundly challenging. We each choose to claim, and live by, the incredibly powerful, core, loving principle....... "All Life Is Sacred"....Sacred...meaning worthwhile, important, valuable, precious, worthy of love, respect, dignity, awe and wonder. This also translates into this new perspective that I'm no better, no worse than that insect, the Land, that tree, that Woman, that child.....**ALL Life Is Sacred.** Once we live by the love principle, all of the poisonous "isms" would die out. The sacred inter-connectedness of all life...takes center stage..... we literally live by the idea of **"All interconnected, All One".** This has always been a core spiritual principle. Now, the science of quantum mechanics demonstrates that at a cellular and molecular level, all of our cells and molecules are always changing and intersecting with all others. So we literally are, all connected and all one.

From the Lakota Native Spiritual Tradition...Mitakuye Oyasin (pronounced – mee tock o yay – o yah sin), meaning "All My Relatives, All My Relations, "We Are All Related... All One"...Each One my Sister, Each One my Brother....The Animals Are My Relatives...The Trees....All part of the Sacred Circle Of Life, The Sacred Hoop...Mother Earth, Father Sky, Grandfather Rocks, Wind Spirits, Thunder Beings....all Guides and Teachers from the Great Beyond....All To Be Honored and Cherished...and All to live with in Harmony. So I do my best to Be Grateful for the Sacred Gift Of Life, and for all the Gifts...My Relatives....and choose to release differences and judgments of myself and all others.

*"Lose all differentiation between myself and others, fit to serve others I will be.*
*And when in serving others I win success, then will I meet the Buddha..*
*and we will smile"*
*-Milarepa, The Great Yogi of Tibet*

*"You will treat the alien who resides with you no differently than the natives*
*born among you; you shall love the alien as yourself; for you too were*
*once aliens in the land".*
*- (NIV)Leviticus 19:33-44*

So if this was the core guiding principle which drives the purpose, the vision and mission statements of every school and church, and all the other institutions in our country... and the world...imagine...please imagine....the affect and effect on all of our children, and their children's children for the next seven generations to come......We will treat ourselves and each other with utmost gentleness, kindness honesty, respect, fairness. Because we are all in this together...we do not see anyone as an adversary in competition for a little piece of the pie. There is plenty to go around for everyone to have a high quality of life, when we choose to live with utmost mutual regard for the sacredness of all beings.

This is a system of values which is in **everyone's** best interest... individually and collectively. Of course, this would require a full-on **agreement**....and full-on **commitment...** by everyone. A **100% commitment** to being our best, with complete honesty and compassion in every thought, word and action, in how we treat ourselves and each other. A high bar to live by ....to be sure. And yet.....we would have soooo much to gain....every one of us. And living by this guiding principle of the sacredness of all life creates this incredible opportunity for "**Loving** Thy Neighbor **As Thyself**". That's it. As simple as I can put it.

So now, a little more about this thing called **Love**.

# Love

Since the beginning, all the wise ones have said .....Love **Is** the answer.

**So, what is this elusive butterfly called Love?**

**As the inimitable Tina Turner sang...** *"What's Love Got To Do With It?"*.......the answer......Everything!

The most powerful force in the universe is LOVE! Always has been, always will be. We humans just forget. And to be fair, it's mostly because we haven't really been taught about love......not nearly as we need to be. The word is thrown around so carelessly, most often without really even knowing what we mean by it. *"It's just a feeling....can't really be explained....but you know it when you feel it"*......like that. Talk about bogus. We've been brainwashed, bamboozled, hoodwinked......to desperately seek this ....thing......that we can't even describe......and we wonder why so many relationships with ourselves and each other end up not feeling fulfilled. <u>As the wise and courageous activist and writer bell hooks (lower case, her preference) so heart-fully teaches us in her wonderful book "All About Love".....we need to define the core values of love (my words, not hers), and then we can create lives filled with those values. Values like gentleness, kindness, commitment, integrity, courage, vulnerability, dependability, fairness, compassion,</u>

**understanding, responsibility, respect, gratitude, trust, and being willing to support ourselves and each other in our mutual spiritual growth. Spiritual growth, for me, implies a life-long learning adventure in deepening my inter-connectedness with all other life, so that we may best serve all others.**

So we're not talking about mamby pamby, goo-goo, ga-ga fantasy love, we're talking about the real deal....fierce, active, passionate, clear, on solid ground LOVE. And it has to start with us being taught about how to honor, and cherish, respect, and care for **ourselves**. And holding ourselves to the highest and most honorable standards of human decency and fairness. If we are willing to bravely venture into this adventure in learning how to love ourselves....and to share that with others as we grow......which, to me, is the main purpose for our being born,.....then all good things are possible.

**So there you have it sports fans! That, to me, is the essence to our living harmoniously with ourselves and each other, on our Sacred Mother Earth. The question then becomes... if we agree, in principle about the aforementioned core values of the sacredness of all life, and of living in love as the blueprint for honoring the sacred....then what are we willing to do about it?**

**For me it's all about the powerful word......
"COMMITMENT". Am I....Are You....Are We....each individually...and collectively......ready.....willing.....and able to commit to living our lives in beauty...walking the**

Sacred path of Love....in all of our thoughts, words and actions........... ...individually and collectively? If we are.... we can fix the problems we've co-created......if we are not..... then we will continue to have the unfulfilling existence we have. Again, commitment, to me, means....100%...all in... not 99%....for that 1% will sabotage our best efforts. That doesn't mean we will do it all perfectly...that's not the point. It's that when we mess up, which we will....no big drama, no excuses.....just, pick ourselves up, dust ourselves off, look honestly and humbly at what we missed that created the misstep, acknowledge it, come up with a better strategy for fixing it expediently, and then carry through with a sustainable plan. In Twelve Step Programs we call it taking a fearless and searching moral inventory and making amends, and committing to and following through on real change. This is similar to the Truth and Conciliation process which so many individuals, families, communities, nations have used to great avail. (Please refer back to some of my prior poems and pieces on truth and conciliation if you're interested in reviewing a little bit more about these and other similar, complementary processes).

I don't know about you...but I'm ready, willing and able to commit to co-creating the amazing life here, and around the world, that I believe we were all put here to live. I hope and pray, that you are too....and that is why you are still reading this.

**Real love is humble, and gentle and kind, courageous, and impeccably honest.** The following are guides to live by, to create inner well-being and outer well-being for us all. So let's look at some of the core ingredients of love and what they represent, (at least to me). And as we explore these core values more and more, it becomes clearer how they each intersect with and complement each other:

*"Out of the Indian approach to life there came a great freedom – an intense and absorbing love for nature; a respect for life; enriching faith in a Supreme Power; and principles of truth, honesty, generosity, equity, and brotherhood as a guide to relations".*
**Luther Standing Bear (1868-1939)**
**Oglala Lakota chief**

~

So let's look at some of the core ingredients of love and what they represent, (at least to me)

And as we explore these core values more and more, it becomes clearer how they each intersect with and complement each other:

# Core Love Values

**Courage**- The willingness to lean into the difficult challenges of life, to Be, and to Do the "right thing". Even in the midst of others' disapproval. A great guiding question for any quandary in life is.... "What would love do now?" "What would be the most loving thing I can do for myself in this situation....that little still voice of truth inside, will always guide us home.....to love....if it doesn't feel right, then the guide isn't love, it's usually fear or guilt. Really important to keep re-learning about that distinction. Are we willing to be courageous enough to be vulnerable...with our feelings....this is the mark of a true love warrior.

**Honesty**- A strong promise to ourselves to act and speak with authenticity. No white lies. When we "get over" on others we're really getting over on ourselves. No way we can feel good about ourselves without living honestly. "The truth **will** set us free". Which is why it is so essential to live by this core value. Lest we be imprisoned by our secrets. "We are as sick as our secrets" (from 12 Step Principles).

**Integrity**- Living with a strong sense of justice and fairness. We live congruently....our behaviors match our values. And again, a willingness to speak up and take action when we see or feel inequity and injustice. Living with impeccable honesty and integrity frees us to live in peace with ourselves, and to feel a deep sense of respect and acceptance.

**Kindness** - We treat ourselves, and others with gentleness, compassion, generosity, empathy, understanding, support. Again, it is crucial that our relationship with ourselves is based on utmost kindness. Otherwise our treatment of others, will likely fall short, and ring hollow, eventually, even leading to resentment and sabotage. Are thoughts and actions reflect our desire for the well-being of ourselves and all others.

**Commitment** - We consistently follow through on our promises to ourselves and others, especially when the going gets tough. And with all these, when we fall short, no big drama, no beating ourselves up, compassionately acknowledging where we went wrong, and revising strategies that are perhaps more realistic and more sustainable.

**Dependability** - We do what we say, and say what we do. Similar to integrity. We believe and have faith in ourselves, because we carry through on our commitments...first and foremost with ourselves, and of course also with others.

**Responsibility** - We take pride in being accountable to ourselves, first and foremost...honoring our most important love priorities in self-care, and the care of others. Being responsible for our well-being fills us with a sense of contentment and peace, since we know we are "taking care of business". Having clear boundaries is very important. If we don't know what our limits are, and don't honor them, we can become resentful, and being doing things out of guilt and fear, not love.

**Fairness/Equity/Equality** – We treat ourselves and others with a sense of fairness, equity and justice. We do our best to ensure equal and fair access to life necessities for all, economically.. food, clothing, shelter, educationally, healthcare...a desirable quality of life for all. If one of us is suffering, it hurts our common humanity. Again, there is plenty to go around if we live by fair and just standards.

**Patience and Acceptance** – We do our best in all of our thoughts words and actions to be very patient with our imperfections, and to hold ourselves and others with unconditional positive regard. We do our best to check our judgments of ourselves, to treat ourselves fairly. And we strive to do the same with others, by trying to put ourselves in their shoes. While this can be extremely difficult....like with all of these values, it can also be extremely rewarding, as it gives the best chance of interconnecting with others who may seem different than us.

**Trust** - Trust takes time to build for ourselves and others. When we consistently demonstrate over time, that we are trustworthy, that is true to our word, then trust becomes a great gift we give ourselves and others. When trust is broken, this is how we determine our willingness to recommit to our core principles. We can do this by carefully accessing what let to the break in trust, and what needs to happen to regain the trust for ourselves and the other. A sincere, heartfelt amends, when appropriate can be very helpful. And then following through on well-thought out strategies to make things right for ourselves and with others (ideally, vetted by the injured party). And of course, consistently carrying through on our commitments to change, and monitored over time. If need be, reassessing and altering strategies as needed.

**Respect** – Treating ourselves and others in the way we would like to be treated. Being respectful and considerate of our and others' feelings, and needs, as consistent with our core values of love and sacredness of all life. Respecting all boundaries, especially sexual ones. Treating ourselves and each other with dignity and reverence for each one's worth. This can be especially difficult when there is significant disagreement, Yet, most disagreements can come to fair and equitable resolution, if both parties are committed to treating each other with respect and kindness, and a willingness to meet in the place of equity and fairness.

**Gratitude/Affection** – Wise elders often say that gratitude is one of the most important love values there is, and can be a true source of genuine affection which we all so greatly need. Affirming and acknowledging our self care, along with our gratitude to the other, can be beautiful and heart filling gifts which make a huge impact on our mental, emotional, spiritual, physical and social well-being.

And relationships individually and collectively can prosper and grow through this simple act of loving expression.

**Spiritual Growth** - **Willingness to nurture spiritual growth in self and others** - When we choose to believe in and live by a belief in the core worth of ourselves and others, and of our inter-connectedness to all things, then our life becomes a reflection of that core value, by how we treat ourselves and each other in our daily lives. Decision making about the most simple, and the most difficult challenges becomes more achievable as our confidence grows through the experience of our spiritual growth.

# Core Love Values Inventories

Using the Core Love Values Listed Above, please consider filling out the following two Core Love Values Inventories For Self and Others, and for Leaders, Institutions and Organizations. For the second inventory, you might start out by picking one leader, institution or organization that moves you to want to take action, and see what comes up for you. (Institutions and organizations may include any groups such as schools (especially teaching accurate history), healthcare, wildlife, environment, churches, business, police/prisons (of course would include treatment of inmates), military, government (especially promoting truth and conciliation processes), and others. In service of all the people, all leaders, institutions and organizations would optimally be reviewed internally and externally (perhaps by unbiased, carefully selected, civilian review boards) for realistic compliance and sustainability on an annual or bi-annual basis. And, for example, a mailer could be sent to cross sections of the state populations or townships asking for feedback using the inventories for whichever leaders institutions/organizations are up for review. Feedback could then be summarized and used for regular review and planning sessions. Citizen ownership would then be a vital, ongoing, mutually advantageous process. Data from both inventories help us determine what is working, and improving what needs improving. This is not about being adversarial with ourselves or others, it's about working together for optimal outcomes for all.

| All Citizen's Core Love Values Inventory For Self and Others* | | | |
|---|---|---|---|
| Core Value | Rate how treat self/others from 1-10(10 being optimal) Self/Others | Describe recent time demonstrated that value Self / Others | Describe specific plan to improve that value Self / Others |
| Courage | | | |
| Honesty | | | |
| Integrity | | | |
| Kindness | | | |
| Commitment | | | |
| Dependability | | | |
| Responsibility | | | |
| Fairness/Equity Equality | | | |
| Patience/ Acceptance | | | |
| Trust | | | |
| Respect | | | |
| Gratitude/ Affection | | | |
| Cooperation/ Service/Sharing | | | |
| Spiritual Growth | | | |

*Based on Fearless and Searching, Kind Moral Inventory from Schiraldi, G. R. (2011), *The Complete Guide to Resilience: Why It Matters; How to Build and Maintain It*. Ashburn, VA: Resilience Training International. © 2011 Glenn R. Schiraldi, Ph.D. Not to be reproduced without written permission** *Human Options*. Toronto: George J. McLeod Limited, 1981, p. 45.

(Altered with permission)

| Core Value | All Citizens' Core Love Values Inventory For Leaders, Institutions, Organizations* | | | | | | | | |
|---|---|---|---|---|---|---|---|---|---|
| | Rate how leader treats employees and public from 1-10 (10 being optimal) | | Rate how Inst./Org. treats employe/pub. (from 1-10) | | Describe recent time demonstrated that value | | Describe specific plan to improve that value | | |
| | Emp | Pub | Emp | Pub | Leader | Inst./Org. | Lead. | Inst./Org. | |
| Courage | | | | | | | | | |
| Honesty | | | | | | | | | |
| Integrity | | | | | | | | | |
| Kindness | | | | | | | | | |
| Commitment | | | | | | | | | |
| Dependability | | | | | | | | | |
| Responsibility | | | | | | | | | |
| Fairness/Equity Equality | | | | | | | | | |
| Patience/ Acceptance | | | | | | | | | |
| Trust | | | | | | | | | |
| Respect | | | | | | | | | |
| Gratitude/ Affection | | | | | | | | | |
| Cooperation/ Serv./Sharing | | | | | | | | | |
| Spirit.Growth | | | | | | | | | |

*Based on Fearless and Searching, Kind Moral Inventory from Schiraldi, G. R. (2011), *The Complete Guide to Resilience: Why It Matters; How to Build and Maintain It.* Ashburn, VA: Resilience Training International. © 2011 Glenn R. Schiraldi, Ph.D. Not to be reproduced without written permission** *Human Options.* Toronto: George J. McLeod Limited, 1981, p. 45.

(Altered with permission)

# Tree Of Living Love

**The following is a visual representation of the Tree Of Living Love – a symbol of the mutual commitment to live and nurture ourselves and each other... All life. One way to view this is to** envision a truth and conciliation process, that is, speaking the truth about our history, and seeing it all, through the eyes of a gardener and the garden of life. We live in a beautiful garden. There are many gorgeous flowers and plants of all colors and shapes. There are also invasive and aggressive weeds that may look attractive, however, left unattended, may drain the soil of it's nutrients, and overpower and suffocate the natural healthy and balanced growth of all of the flowers and plants. It may be noted, that the poison of some of the weeds, blended with the sweet pollen of some of the flowers and plants, can have powerful healing properties. So the gardeners need to first learn about and recognize the poisonous roots of decay. And then the garden needs continuous, vigilant weeding and tilling and revitalizing of the soil to maintain the precious life affirming balance.

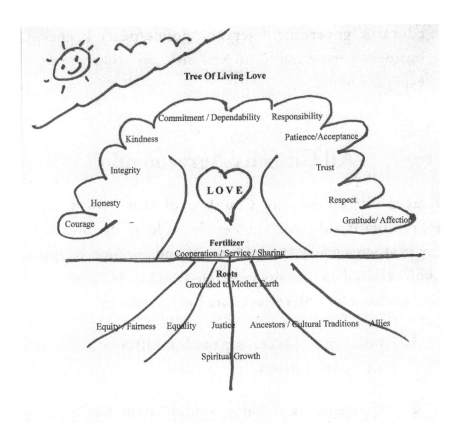

**Tree Of Living Love**

Commitment / Dependability    Responsibility

Kindness    Patience/Acceptance

Integrity    Trust

**LOVE**

Honesty    Respect

Courage    Gratitude/ Affection

**Fertilizer**
Cooperation / Service / Sharing

**Roots**
Grounded to Mother Earth

Equity / Fairness    Equality    Justice    Ancestors / Cultural Traditions    Allies

Spiritual Growth

# Commitment Proposal

It is proposed, that every citizen will sign and commit to live by the following agreement(whether born here or not... refugee, immigrant, young, old, gay, straight, parent, child, blue color worker, white color worker, educator, government servant, police/peace keeper, business person,...and on and on)....in other words, everyone of us.

# All Citizens' Agreement*

I, as a citizen of this Country, of this World, as a representative of ...All The People....Pledge my life, to do my best with every thought, word and action... to make choices based on the core belief that All Life Is Sacred, and that each choice will reflect core Love values by:

1.  Checking and accessing my commitment with each core value as listed

2.  Expressing each value commitment out loud to myself, and ideally to another I feel responsible to

3.  Continuing to reassess my commitment of my pledge to myself and the others I serve, through regularly scheduled written and spoken self-reflection

4. Committing to maintain regularly scheduled, mutually agreed upon reviews with those I serve

5. Signing my name as my promise to live by each value

This is my word.

**Signed**
*(It is recommended that a yearly day of celebration be initiated to honor every citizen's living by their sacred pledge).*

# Native

I embrace Being Born of the Sweet Mother Earth

I embrace Being Child I embrace Being Adult

I embrace Being Female I embrace Being Male

I embrace Being 79, at least in this life

I embrace Being Italian, Francesco Roberto Vincenzo Schiraldi, roots in Palo del Colle, and Marsico Nuovo (just wish my parents spoke Italian at home, not only when we went to my grandparents), and I honor my ancestors (and yours), and the history and traditions we lost ...in order to "assimilate")

I embrace Being from Brooklyn and East Rockaway

I embrace Being working class.....and educated.

I embrace having these dark skin pigmentations- "beauty marks" (as my grandma called them)...all over my contrasting lighter skinned body.

I embrace Breathing.......And invite us all to Breathe.....

I embrace Being Lakota

I embrace Being African

I embrace Being Latino

I embrace Being Asian

I embrace Being 2 Spirit/Gay/Trans/Straight

I embrace Being able bodied and having disabilities

I embrace Being The Butterfly, The Buffalo, The Gorilla, The Lilac, The Mountain, The Ocean, The Fire, The Sky

I embrace Being Unique....I embrace Being Connected to the Heart of Each of You......

I embrace Being One, With All Life, and.. Breathing...Being Fully Committed to uncovering the wealthy, white, hetero, male supremacy cultural values conditioning in me.. and in all of us....

…... Breathing....Being Imperfect and Willing to keep learning from my mistakes in doing this difficult work, with courage, integrity, gentleness.

I embrace Being Alive....... I embrace Being Me.. Here with You.

Pilamaya, Grazie
FRVS / Summer 02, revised 10/14,12/24

# Two-Spirit*

Walking a spiritual path of healing, light and love, embracing and embodying a deep connection with the universal tones and energies of the Sacred Feminine and the Sacred Masculine, all in one body, one mind, one spirit.

| Sacred Feminine | Sacred Masculine |
|---|---|
| Mother Earth | Father Sky |
| Place of: | Place of: |
| nurturance | warrior |
| gentleness | strength |
| kindness | courage |
| forgiveness | perseverance |
| comfort | protection |
| compassion | impeccable honesty |
| humility | dependability |
| acceptance | equality/equity |

*This is what I learned from my teachers during my preparation for and participation in many healing ceremonies of the Sicangu, Lakota, on the Rosebud Reservation in Little White River, South Dakota.

Most of our teaching came from Tom Balistrieri who was an apprentice to Joe Eagle Elk, a very revered and respected Iyeska (medicine man) on the Rosebud. While many Lakota, understandably, do not want whites to participate in their sacred ceremonies, Joe Eagle Elk felt that it was important for whites to learn the traditions (as long as done very respectfully), if real healing was to happen. Our tiopaye/family group of college counselors from around the country, was invited by Harold Whitehorse, a Sicangu Chief to attend the sacred Sundance ceremony because we had been trained very carefully about how to respect the Lakota spiritual traditions. For eight years I was blessed to attend the sacred Sundance ceremony, as well as completed my four year hanblecya (vision quest) and agreed to a life long commitment to be a pipe carrier (using the pipe I was given by Harold Whitehorse, to do healing ceremony).

Amongst the Sicangu, the two-spirit hold a place of honor, respected as powerful, highly intuitive healers because of their deep connection with the mother earth and father sky. Depending on which tribe they were part of, two-spirit were often ostracized and persecuted, even killed. I relate this to witches being burned because of their powerful connection to nature. We had special ceremonies to honor those who chose to claim our own two-spirit, and for our two-spirit sisters and brothers, who have been killed and suffer because of who they are. A small group of our tiospaye claimed our two-spirit in special ceremony.

I believe that at our core, we are all two-spirit. Unfortunately due to fear, we are taught to choose between our feminine and masculine energies. While two-spirit is not necessarily about sexual orientation, expressing our healthy feminine and masculine sexual energy and passion is certainly an important part of healing, joyful, harmonious life. I believe that racism, homophobia, and all the "isms" would be healed if we each embraced our two-spirit.

Hope this helps.
I am honored to know you.
Mitakuye oyasin (all my relatives),
Francesco Roberto Vincenzo

# My Sacred Feminine

Alive
In me
Is the
Miracle
Of Life.
Continually
Being reborn
Renewing
Recreating
Nurturing
Sustaining
Energy.
Compassionate
Soothing
Comfort.
Forgiving
Humility.
Healing
The wounds
Deep
To the core
Of Mother Earth
Of me.
A gentle
Salve
Washing over
The scars.

Joyfully
Pronouncing
Freedom.

FRS/12/06

~

**The Creator, Great Spirit, Wakantanka, The Universal One**, never fails to remind me of the sacred, loving path, and the ongoing work to restore balance.

- My cherished teacher of the Lakota traditions, Tom/Rags sent two beautiful passages to me about the importance of the two-spirited ones (who embody the greatest qualities of the sacred feminine and sacred masculine, all in one), and who are beautiful, healing empaths for us to turn to for wisdom, healing, guidance.

- Another grueling, agonizing pipeline protest by brave Indigenous People and their supporters, to prevent further illegal desecration of sacred lands.

-**My beloved friend and brother John invited me to accompany him in support of some distinguished Lakota Elders who are part of a delegation traveling east to retrieve the remains of Lakota children who died at one of the first Indian boarding schools. The children had been forced to leave their families and tribes (to be "assimilated", "kill the Indian, save the man"), often treated horrifically, many never seeing their loved ones again. Their families and tribes had been previously prevented from taking their remains home. Now, over a hundred years later, they can be brought home. The wounds so deep...so deep. Yet, finally, maybe now, their spirits can be free. And a little healing can start.**

*For a moment....if you would.....please take a deep breath...close your eyes... and try to imagine how you would feel... in your heart and body.... if one of these children.... is your child.*

# The Children

Oh... the Children.
their spirits
yearning to be free.

Finally they can return
home again
to their loved ones.

And their spirits
can continue
on their sacred journey.


Honoring Our Children
.....from the plantations
.....from the boarding schools
.....in the border detention centers
.....in human trafficking
All of our children, everywhere
For seven generations to come.

All children want to know..
Am I loved?
Will I be comforted?
Is the world safe?
The answers determine
a kinder world.

In saving our children,

We save our country.

In saving our children,
We save our world.

In saving our children,
We save...ourselves.

Honoring the children
through loving action
is how we can re-create
a loving world.

Mitakuye Oyasin
All My Relatives


Please keep the spirits of the young ones, who have suffered so much, in your loving hearts and prayers ..... their families and loved ones, .... the elders who continue this difficult healing work.... and all those who work to make it right.

~

*"When the first chakra is disconnected from the feminine Earth, we can feel orphaned and motherless. We look for security from material things. Individuality prevails over relationships, and selfish drives triumph over family, social and global responsibility. The more separated we become from the Earth, the more hostile we become to the feminine. We disown our passion, our creativity, and our sexuality. Eventually, the Earth itself becomes a baneful place. I remember being told by a medicine woman in the Amazon, "Do you know why they are really cutting down the rain forest? Because it is wet and dark and tangled and feminine"*
**- Alberto Villoldo, Ph.D,**
**Dance of the Four Winds: Secrets of**
**the Inca Medicine Wheel.**
*(With loving appreciation, once again, to my dear friend and colleague Dr. Maria del Carmen Rodriguez, for sending the above quote to me, and for her loving help with editing this essay.)*

~

*Please see <u>"America Needs A Woman President", by Brett Bevill, drawings by Eben Dodd,</u> a wise and moving little book which really gets to the heart of our huge need for more Women in leadership positions, especially Black, Indigenous, LGBTQ2S, and Women of Color, who live and lead by the core sacred love values previously discussed.*

~

*"I am going to venture that the man who sat on the ground in his tipi meditating on life and its meaning, accepting the kinship of all creatures, and acknowledging unity with the universe of things, was infusing into his being the true essence of civilization."*
**Luther Standing Bear (1868?-1939)**
**Oglala Lakota chief.**

~

*"You might say I'm a dreamer,*
*but I'm not the only one.*
*I hope some day you'll join us,*
*And the world will be as one"*
*-"Imagine"*
*John Lennon*

~

# Dear Ones,

May our heart-felt choices
to share our love with each other,
be the healing we all so long for.

May we each cherish
the Sacred in us,
and all things.

May we each walk
in love and beauty,
as we make our way
back home again.

Roberto

# I Wish You Love.....

### I Wish You Peace

### I Wish You Safety

### I Wish You Joy

### I Wish You Health

### I Wish You Acceptance

### I Wish You Respect

### <u>I WISH YOU LOVE</u>

# Additional Author Information

Dr. Roberto Schiraldi, EdD, LCP, LCADC is a licensed professional counselor, licensed clinical alcohol and other drug counselor, and has been a racial justice advocate, trainer, and trauma therapist for over 40 years. Roberto is retired from Counseling and Psychological Services at Princeton University, where he was coordinator of the alcohol and other drug treatment team, and was previously employed in a similar capacity by Temple University, where he received his doctorate in Holistic Health Education and Counseling. He is a past President of the New Jersey Association for Multicultural Counseling, past Co-Chair of the Ethics Committee of the New Jersey Counseling Association, and has been a member of numerous racial justice organizations, boards, and committees. He is a pipe carrier in the Sicangu Lakota Native Spiritual Healing Tradition, a Vietnam era veteran, and member of Veterans For Peace.

~

*To contact me, please go to my website www.robertoschiraldi. com, (with related racial justice podcast interviews, and information on how to order my other books, and two abridged audio books, both recorded in my voice (each approx. two hours long), one on 'Healing Love Poems for white supremacy culture', and the most recent one, on 'Awakening With Love').*

Printed in the United States
by Baker & Taylor Publisher Services